Merry Christmas Sylvia from Laurel (& Wendy)

We Came to Say

A Collection of Memoir

Twenty-Six Pieces from Writers Who've Worked with Theo Pauline Nestor

Edited by
Theo Pauline Nestor

Permissions

"No Man's Land" by Lauren McGuire was originally published in the Winter 2008 issue of *No Touching, A Literary Magazine of Literary Nonfiction.*

"Maria" by Richard Rodgers and Oscar Hammerstein II Copyright © 1959 by Richard Rodgers and Oscar Hammerstein II. Used by Permission of Williamson Music, A Division of Rodgers & Hammerstein: An Imagem CompanyCopyright Renewed. International Copyright Secured. All Rights Reserved.

Cover illustration used with permission of the artist, Anthony Russo © 2011

ISBN: 978-1-60944-027-5

 Designed, printed, and bound by Vladimir Verano at Third Place Press, Lake Forest Park, on the Espresso Book Machine v.2.2.
thirdplacepress.blogspot.com

For Kumi and all the rest of my students
Your courage inspires me.

Table of Contents

Introduction

As I set out to introduce the writers included here, my first impulse was to tell you how I met them, what teaching has meant to me, and how watching my students grow has given me the courage to write deeper, further, to believe in my own voice and the power of memoir just that much more.

"See," my inner Iago then hissed. "*See* how you always make it about *you?* Step aside for once." Chastened, I sat down at the keyboard with the directive to "step aside" firmly in mind. Make it about them! Over the next few days, I started three different introductions with a shame simmering inside me; my first impulse had been wrong. My three attempts read something like the worst imaginable state of the nation addresses. All generalities about memoir and no heart.

I share this struggle with you—and yes, I made it about me! again!—because it is the very struggle I've watched many of my memoir writing students go through—the struggle between the desire to tell your own story and the competing internal force that asserts that no good will ever come from this, that precious time is being wasted. It's a voice certain that memoir writing is self-indulgent, self-aggrandizing, self-pitying, and just downright selfish. It sounds a little like the voice of your ninth grade grammar teacher or maybe what we've been led to believe is the voice of reason. But the longer I'm involved with memoir, the more I'm convinced that the voice is wrong and that it is through our own stories that we come to connect to each other. When we follow the path of our own very particular stories of loss and triumph, we find the road into the common human story. In fact, it is through coming to know ourselves that we come to know others. So, instead of gazing into our own navels—as some critics would assert—I say we are gazing into the greater navel.

So, let's forget all that state of the nation stuff. Let me tell you my story of how I came to know and work with these students. Five years ago, I walked into my first "Writing the Memoir" class at the University of Washington, thinking it was a job. I was working on a memoir of my own, and in my mind, the writing was the important work and the teaching was a bill-paying job, teaching writing a few hours a week to busy professionals.

But each September, I received a new group of "busy professionals," and by Christmas they'd have morphed into a room full of individuals with stories of grace, loss and regret not visible at first glance, unfolding stories that bound me to their creators. Each June, I've watched yet another group of students take to the podium at the University Bookstore, reading their work in steady voices to each other, their loved ones, and a few stray Tuesday night shoppers.

It was also around five years ago that I started my work as a "writing coach," a job I'd never had dreamed existed before the first time I found myself in a café with an emerging writer who bought me a cup of coffee and said she'd give me twenty dollars to tell her what I thought of her short stack of pages. Is this *legal*? I thought. But newly divorced mother of two that I was, I downed the cup of coffee and got busy. I left an hour later thinking I might be onto something. Could I "coach" writers? It turns out I could. A few months later, I hosted a writers' retreat up on Orcas Island (a few of the writers in this anthology were there that weekend), and I took the ferry back to Seattle a few days later with a vision for how I wanted to work with writers outside of the classroom setting. I knew I wanted to have an ongoing relationship with my writing students. I wanted to watch them grow and evolve. I wanted to see where their stories would go.

And now, some years later, I'm excited to have this chance to watch these writers come into print—some for the first time, some not. Many of these writers were in the "Writing the Memoir" class at UW and some I've worked with individually. Some have come to my house on Saturday mornings to eat scones and work on their stories. All have struggled and triumphed.

Introduction

I wish there were a word that was like "proud" that was better than "proud." Proud plus joyful plus respect. Does that make sense? But, I'll make do with proud. I'm proud of these writers; it is a joy to know them, and I so respect this work and where it takes us. All of us.

Theo Pauline Nestor
Seattle
March, 2011

Where Do You Go?

By Jennifer Landau

My son Adam wants to know if our dog is going to die soon. Adam's nearly nine and has never asked about death, so I'm thrown.

"I hope not," I say, which I know will get me nowhere. Adam has autism so when he asks questions, he wants specifics: names, dates, places. He's like the guys from *Dragnet* in camouflage board shorts.

"Yes or no?" he asks.

Our dog Max is fourteen, so "yes." But I don't want to say that, don't want follow-up questions about where we go when we die and what happens when we get there and whether we'll see the dog again.

I hadn't planned for this. I'd been too busy with the Lazy Susan that is life with autism: One week Adam is bounding out of bed at six a.m. The next week I have to drag him out at eight. He's afraid of pigeons; no, it's wind chimes, then back to pigeons. He can be surly and weepy and high as a kite, often on the same day.

On top of that, I'm a single mom, having had Adam through donor insemination when I was pushing forty and not long out of another failed relationship. There just isn't much time to ponder philosophical issues. I don't even know where Adam heard about death. Can I blame *SpongeBob* for this? When in doubt, I like to blame *SpongeBob*.

I distract Adam by telling him he can play with his Nintendo Wii, and then run to call my friend Laura. I met Laura when we moved from New York City to the surrounding suburbs to be closer to my family after Adam's diagnosis. She has a daughter on the autism spectrum and the two of us seem to freak out on opposite days, as if we have that, along with everything else, tightly scheduled.

"Death," I say, as soon as she picks up. With limited time, I need to cut to the chase.

"Is that a request?" she asks. "Because I'm not down with that, Hon."

"Adam's asking about death," I say. "About the dog dying, specifically."

"Well, that's good," she says. "That's a normal thing to ask about."

"But I have no answer."

"Just tell him whatever you believe," she says.

Oy.

I don't know what I believe. It's not that I gave up on God because my son has autism. In fact, it's having Adam that's made me question my lazy mix of quasi-Jewiness and "meh" agnosticism. One look at that kid's face and you've got to have faith in something.

Although both my parents are Jewish, I wasn't raised with any religious education. We rarely went to temple, and when my two older sisters quit Hebrew school, I never got the chance to go. We even had a fake Christmas tree, this huge silver mess that I'm sure was loaded with lead.

I never questioned why we had a tree. I think my mother wanted the holidays to be "fun" and my father was a bit self-hating—he thought doing well meant putting aside old-timey things like culture and religion. When I was working on some school project and asked him what our background was, he said, "American." He worshipped success: his big house and big Cadillac, and family trips to California, where we'd play elevator tag at the Century Plaza.

Most years Mom would set up the Menorah, though if Hanukkah fell far from Christmas, she sometimes forgot. She'd clean out last year's wax with the tines of a fork and lead the three of us in the blessing. (Dad was always working late.) Instead of saying "Baruch Atah Adoni," my sisters would joke and say, "Baruch had toys, I don't know…" Mom would shush them and remind us that it was important to have some respect for our traditions.

I've followed pretty much the same routine, though we go to my parents for Christmas, and they no longer put up a tree. There are special education Hebrew school classes, but they haven't felt like a priority to me, not when Adam still can't get a dental checkup without having to be sedated or read at grade level.

As for death, Mom's running joke is that she wants to leave this earthly realm in a Hefty bag. "Just remember," she'll say. "Tuesday is trash day."

Actually, she wants to be cremated, though I think that might be against Jewish law. My father wants to be buried. It seems fitting that they'd be at odds about this, too, though they do want to be interred in the same plot.

I tell my mother about this graveside monument I saw in Vermont, a huge sculpture of a husband and wife holding hands and the words "set me as a seal upon thine heart for love is strong as death."

"Well, now don't be ridiculous," she says.

Personally, I'd like to be cremated and have my ashes scattered over some of Adam's favorite haunts so I know he'd be back to visit. That might not go over too well with the folks in the produce department at Whole Foods, though in my defense I am both local and organic.

Adam wakes up five times that night, which is not unusual for him. I give up on staying in my room and form a ball at the bottom of his twin bed. Adam's eyes are puffy and his hair looks like the four leaves of a ceiling fan.

"I don't want Max to die!" he says.

"He's fine, honey," I say. "He's snoring away in the living room."

By the next morning, Adam is on to other things, but I'm thinking ahead since I know that Lazy Susan will spin again. What *will* I do when the dog dies? Maybe burying him in the pet cemetery a few towns away would be a decent way to introduce Adam to the rituals of death.

I phone the pet cemetery and speak to a woman who barrels through her sales pitch with cheery determination. She says that I can purchase a pre-needs plot and then starts going on about pastoral care and lawn maintenance programs and a bunch of other stuff that probably adds up to thousands of dollars.

"Um, this is for a dog," I say, before hanging up.

I head to the library to see if there's a book that might help. There's one that talks about how plants and animals and people all have beginnings and endings and that it's the time in the middle that we call living. While I appreciate that there's no particular religious slant to the book, I think reminding Adam that flowers and rabbits and lady-bugs all die will turn the natural world into one big horror show for him.

When the book mentions that people get sick, it says that they usually get better—but sometimes they don't. The picture that accompanies this reassuring idea shows a boy wincing as he has a splinter removed. All I need is Adam thinking that his life is over every time I reach for the tweezers.

Another book is called *Heaven for Kids,* and I can't tell if it's a parody because each chapter opens with quotes from both the *Bible* and *The Chronicles of Narnia.* The author says that we should prepare for heaven like we're preparing for a trip to Disney or Six Flags. Does that mean all it takes is sunblock and a good pair of walking shoes?

I don't know if I believe in God, but I do wish I believed in heaven. I get the appeal, the comfort in it, and it would be such an easy sell to an anxious little boy. I suppose I could pretend, like I do about Santa and the Tooth Fairy. But it seems like too big a lie. And if I tell Adam something vague like how we carry the spirits of our dead loved ones with us, he'll want to know if he'd need a bigger backpack for that. Or maybe a wagon would make more sense, and wouldn't it be best to order one soon, as in now, as in "please bring me the catalog"?

Like a lot of kids with autism, Adam is incredibly literal and wedded to his routine. I made a fruit salad the other day and as we sat there sharing it, I realized that he was eating the fruit in alphabetical order. The way his mind works amazes me. Yet his tendency to hang on my every word and action can make me so afraid of a misstep that I'm paralyzed.

I call my sister Wendy, ask her what she told my niece and nephew, who are now in their teens, about death.

"Oh, I have no idea," she says. "They picked it up on the street like everything else."

We joke about this for a while, about kids huddling in corners and whispering things like "and then the man puts the woman in the ground…" or calling out random "nasty" words: *casket, eulogy, internment.*

"We're going to hell for this," she says.

"Do you believe in hell?" I ask.

"Some place you go and burn for eternity? No."

"Heaven?"

"I believe, as that great philosopher Belinda Carlisle once said, that heaven is a place on earth. Ditto, hell."

I question why we never went to visit our father's parents at the cemetery on Long Island. Wendy says that it's a long drive from Westchester and she figures that Mom and Dad never felt the need to look at a headstone to think about his folks. My mother's parents were cremated and there was no memorial service for either of them.

"Do we even know where their ashes are?" I ask.

"Knowing Mom, she's probably got them in a closet somewhere next to a box of Girl Scout Cookies from 1979."

"Oh, my God!" I say. "I forgot about Trixie."

"Your cat?" Wendy asks. "I thought you buried her in a park somewhere."

"But I didn't," I say, and quickly hang up.

I find Trixie's ashes on the highest shelf in my walk-in closet, where I put them the day we moved in six and a half years ago. She'd died when Adam was an infant, a time when I was going through a tough postpartum period and Adam was starting to show early signs of developmental problems. I was too caught up to really grieve for her, though I had loved her dearly. Now I hadn't even remembered that she was here.

Her ashes are in a small round tin with a floral pattern, something you'd use to store hard candies. I open it, lift out a baggie, and notice how much her ashes look like kitty litter.

"Hey, girl," I say, resting the bag on my palm. "Sorry you've been stuck up there."

The thing is, I'd thought about the cat a lot over the years. I just hadn't connected those thoughts to the tin in my closet. When I pictured Trixie, the image was of her lying next to me on the couch kneading my stomach or racing from room to room, her big belly hanging down like an awning. At one point, I'd considered sprinkling her ashes somewhere in Prospect Park because I'd lived in Brooklyn for much of her life and she'd been happy there. I just didn't get around to it, though. I guess I've never been great at dealing with death.

A couple of days go by, and then one night after reading *No, David!* for the twentieth time that week, Adam snuggles next to me on his bed and asks again if the dog is going to die.

"He is very old, honey," I say. "If he were a person he'd be 98 years old, so he's lived a long, long, time."

Adam looks at me with his huge brown eyes, and I think, screw it, if he asks what happens after we die, I'll go for the heaven angle. Is it that much worse than telling him there's some winged creature that comes into his bedroom in the middle of the night and takes his *teeth?*

"Then yes?" he asks.

"At some point," I say, and let out a long breath. "Yes."

"And me?" he asks, yanking on his pajama top. "I'm going to die?"

"Not until you're a very, *very* old man, like a hundred years from now. That's a big number, right?"

"Will I have white hair then? Or gray?"

"White, probably. Like Grandpa."

"So first I'll have brown hair, then salt and pepper hair, then gray, then white, and then that's it."

"Sounds about right," I say, touching his cheek.

"And where do I go if you die?"

"Where do *you* go?" I ask. "Oh, you go to live with Aunt Wendy."

"And if she dies?" he asks.

"To Aunt Barbara," I say, referring to my eldest sister.

"Do they know how to operate a microwave oven?" he asks.

"Of course."

"And do they love me?" he asks.

"Very much," I say.

Adam looks down, working his jaw as he contemplates all this. Then he swallows hard and shoves the book into my lap.

"Okay," he says. "Read."

He wakes up only twice that night, which is some sort of record for him.

The next day I spend an hour browsing through this website where you can order customized pet urns. There are a ton of choices, some wood, some metal, some with paw prints, some with figurines on top. It's hard not to laugh at the *Pimp My Urn* absurdity of it all, but there's something really touching about it, too.

I order one for Trixie with her name engraved on it and a spot for her photo. I don't know what I'll tell Adam when it arrives. Like everything else with him, I'll have to figure it out as we go along. But if I get him to understand a little without freaking out a lot, well, most days that's as close to heaven as we get down here.

The Hole

By Paul Boardman

PRINCETON, NEW JERSEY. DECEMBER 16, 1983. It was the last day of seminary classes for the semester. Penny, my first wife, and I would be driving frozen roads for eleven hours back to Holland, Michigan the next day to spend the Christmas holidays with her family, the Vandersteen clan. I was worried about spending all the holiday time with my in-laws. Because I had entered seminary and was now a budding clergyman, I was expected to deliver a devotional thought and to say a profound Grace before every meal.

At twenty-four, I wasn't confident that I was up to the task of playing family spiritual leader. I wasn't really sure about my young marriage either. Penny succumbed to immobilizing migraines weekly, and was always, it seemed, laid low at those times when I was ready to soar. She became debilitated in perfect timing with each of the high moments of my seminary experience: when we arrived at Princeton to take our first tour of the lovely campus; at the formal welcome dinner with faculty for incoming seminarians; at convocation; at the married student housing picnic; on my birthday; hours before I had to deliver my first sermon for homiletics class. I was frustrated and unhappy in my marriage. Her headaches put a space between us and emphasized our lack of common interests. We weren't communicating with each other the way I imagined other married couples were. We weren't growing in the same direction. We clandestinely snuck to marriage counseling off campus, keeping it secret because she didn't think our troubles warranted therapy in the first place, but hidden also because, if we were having any trouble, she didn't want anyone to know.

But my unease regarding the next two weeks with her family was overshadowed by the immediate task of going on my last visitation of the semester to Trenton State Penitentiary. It was the last visit of that first semester, about halfway through my year-long internship as a seminarian chaplain at the locked Unit for the Criminally Insane at the penitentiary. I had deliberately but naively signed up for an untraditional internship; I wanted to avoid the more commonly chosen path of student-pastoring in a church, because I thought that my future ministry would be in the area of social work.

The Unit for the Criminally Insane was located in a separate secure campus within the main Trenton State Penitentiary grounds. The high, windowless red sandstone walls made it look like a cross between a medieval castle and an electrical power station. In the unit where I worked, there was never a moment when the prisoners were in the presence of another human without bars between them. They took showers by themselves, participated in Recreation entirely by themselves. My visits were supposed to provide human contact, conversation and spiritual comfort but from a protective, three-foot distance from the bars of the inmate's cell. I broke these rules sometimes, out of naive solidarity with the inmates. I shook the inmates' hands, from time to time, leaning on the bars, my arms thrust into their cells.

"One last time," I told myself. "Just buck up and get the prison visit over with. And you will be rewarded with a well-deserved two weeks off!"

In our Princeton apartment I put on my starched and stiff clergy's black shirt and inserted the white plastic clerical tab into the collar. I felt the usual same foreboding as I sunk into the cracked vinyl bucket seat of my 1973 Datsun 210 to motor south on New Jersey Route #1 towards Trenton. As I drove, I slowly abandoned the comfortable, verdant, privileged Princeton with its rolling hills, parks and gothic buildings built of brown and grey stone and moved toward Trenton, one of the most blighted cities in America. As I entered Trenton city limits, my dread increased.

When I arrived in the vast parking lot of the prison and parked, I paused to collect myself. With the door slightly ajar and one foot on the pavement, I sat in the driver's seat and conspired how short I could make this visit. On my two previous visits I had worked the upper tiers of the locked units: Tier A and B, with long wide hallways that had windows on one side, 20 cells lining the other. Today, it was my turn to visit The Hole.

The Hole was the name for the cells in the basement that had no windows, the cells where prisoners were sent to be "disciplined," rumor had it, by guards who were punishing the prisoners for assaulting their fellow correction officers (COs). In The Hole, a prison within a prison, the prisoners were stripped of everything. The most violent among them were issued paper gowns. They were angry, from their beatings and their deprivation. They always seemed defiant, seething with explosive rage. The Hole had to be regularly hosed down because COs, or anyone, who walked by the cells might be "shitted." On my first day in The Hole, in September, a guard had planted me at the start of "the gauntlet" and told me not to move. He then jerkily but erratically raced down the hall, demonstrating to me how to dodge being shitted by abruptly alternating his pace to throw off the inmates' timing. The way he so quickly and gracefully moved down the flesh-colored tile hall seemed to me to be a combination of boxing and tap-dancing.

When he returned, clean and unscathed, he said, almost mockingly, "Your turn. Good luck, Father!"

As I ventured down that hall for the first time, I was exceedingly afraid. I tried not to show my panic as I advanced. I only talked to the inmates in the first two cells that day, but I avoided being shitted.

The Hole was where the inmate Holman White, with his vacant stare, seemed to live permanently. He never put on his paper gown but just stood naked and hulking, facing the bars, whenever anyone passed in front of his cell, Cell 3. Every time I saw him he seemed confused, but I couldn't tell whether or not he had become harmless. The year before, Holman White had killed a corrections officer by jamming a stainless steel serving spoon, as long as a man's arm, down the CO's throat and esophagus. After that, an off-the-books beating by the deceased's fellow guards had left White's black face slightly concave on his right temple and permanently asymmetrical. The Hole was a convenient place to keep him, windowless and without visitors, except for a few sanctioned do-gooders like me. White never answered me when I greeted him. I always wondered if he could even speak.

I felt intense unease outside in the prison parking lot but wanted to get this visit over with so my vacation could commence. I slammed the car door with self-bolstered determination, and as I headed through the parking lot I passed two women, older than me, who were returning from a visit with an inmate; perhaps their husband or brother? They giggled as they passed me, as though they had discovered how preposterous I was with my Priest's collar, my fear and my inexperience.

"Hi Father!" they both mocked, in unison.

I nodded in response as I walked down a path lined on both sides by fence with ominous concertina razor wire running atop it. My dread rose as I faced the first pair of gargantuan steel doors.

"How we doin' this fine day, Father?" the grey uniformed Corrections Officer asked cheerfully, when I held up my dangling passes to his guard booth window.

I wasn't sure if I detected a note of sarcasm. He pressed a button that opened the heavy doors with a loud sound that startled me.

To get to The Hole I spent fifteen minutes negotiating long passageways after passing through successive sets of these oppressive steel doors. At each door I had to show my pass. I had never been able to get used to the jarringly loud noise of the steel slamming on steel, tightly locking down. My nerves were jangled by the time I started my "work."

When I got to The Hole's Office, three burly officers were standing there laughing. They said they had just hosed down the hall, Holman White's cell, and Holman White.

"He doesn't even know where the toilet is!" said one, and they all laughed uproariously.

I shifted nervously in the office, wondering which Cell to concentrate on for my visit.

They showed me a list of inmates in the cells and said, "Twitchy just got to The Hole this morning. He might want to talk to you today, Father. He's in Cell 4."

I had talked to Twitchy on Tier B before and wondered what he had done to land himself in The Hole. Probably assault or disrespecting a guard. He was a small, wiry white man with a carefully groomed Fu Manchu mustache. He seemed explosive: His darting eyes and intense nervousness befitted his name. He constantly fingered and twisted the long side bars of his Fu Manchu.

The guards let me through the gate out onto the gauntlet. I walked quickly past Holman White standing still and naked, to Cell 4 and stood in front of the bars. Twitchy rose and greeted me; he seemed almost happy to see me. He was wearing his paper gown. He reached through the bars in an offer to shake my hand. I shook his hand but stepped back to the regulation three feet separation. He then sat on his bed as if inviting me to relax and settle into conversation with him.

I asked Twitchy, "How is it going down here?"

He smiled and looked down, stroking his mustache, "It's all sunshine, Father," he sneered.

His neighbor in Cell 5, obviously listening in, howled. I felt embarrassed at my question and moved in closer to the bars and Twitchy. I felt uneasy being overheard by his neighbors and wanted to speak in a softer voice.

He asked me, looking at my clerical collar skeptically, "Are you really a priest?"

I replied, "No, not yet anyway. I am studying to be a Protestant minister at the theological seminary up in Princeton. Where are you from?" I asked, wanting to change the subject. I was now standing right at the bars that separated us.

Twitchy said, "Asbury Park. Know it?"

I answered, trying to show solidarity, finding a commonality, "Isn't that where Bruce Springsteen is from?"

"You got it." he replied breezily.

I relaxed a little and leaned in resting my forearms on the bars, projecting my arms into his cell. Twitchy rose off his bed quickly and grabbed my left hand and arm that were sticking into his cell, as if to shake my hand.

He gripped my hand and arm firmly, "I want to ask you something, Father. Do you trust me?"

I replied, trying joviality to mask the obvious nervousness in my voice, "Sure, I trust you. But you do have my arm!"

Twitchy tightened his grasp further, then said, "Seriously Father, I want to ask you again, do you really trust me?"

"I do," I said weakly, knowing that the trouble I had gotten myself in was the very reason the prison had the stringent rule not to shake the prisoners' hands in the first place.

"Father, this is a game of trust. I want you to trust me. Because if I wanted to right now I could break your arm off."

I could only try to swallow the rising dry lump of fear in my throat. One of his hands was "hand-shaking" my left hand. His other hand was vice-locked onto the wrist of that hand.

"Are you still trusting me, Father?" he sneered, looking into my eyes demanding an answer.

I eked out a thin, "Yes." I had never been so afraid in my twenty-four years.

"Because we are going to take your trust to a new level. Relax your hand!"

I did as he told. I felt his gnarly hands slide around my gold wedding ring. I clenched my hand again. I knew what he was going to do.

His face clouded, "Father, if you don't relax your hand, I could break your arm off." I knew he was right. "This is a game of trust, remember!"

I felt defeated and finally, relenting, relaxed my hand. He slipped off my wedding band and put it in his mouth.

Immediately, he let go of my hand and arm. "See – trust! I didn't break your arm off! But Father, if you tell the guards, you will be responsible for my beating and anyway you will never get your ring back because you will have to pick through my shit to get it. Thanks for stopping by, Father!"

Twitchy opened his mouth slightly to reveal the glint of gold on his tongue, taunting me.

His neighbor chuckled. I stepped back from the bars and stared at him. I hoped that my trembling was not visible to him.

I said softly, "Merry Christmas," and walked slowly back up to the gate that led out of The Hole.

In the office, one of the CO's said, "That was a short visit, Father! You ok?"

I replied I was fine.

When The Hole door slammed shut behind me I winced. I then walked slowly and heavily down a long echoing passageway. I wondered what I would tell Penny about the missing wedding ring. Its absence seemed a strange omen on my bare hand.

First in Flight

By Jennifer Crowder

WE ARE MARRIED AT TWENTY-FOUR AFTER YOU RETURN from six months in the Sinai, where you'd been part of the Multinational Force and Observers. You loved the vast, spare silence of the Egyptian desert. Yet you wrote of sounds: the cries of the Bedouins herding their goats and the Muslim call to prayer echoing through remote wadis, mixing with the intertwined voices of the violin and cello from the recording of Brahms's Double Concerto I'd sent.

Your two weeks' leave from the Army's 82nd Airborne barely gives us time for the wedding itself before friends and worried parents, a night's stay at Seattle's just-opened Inn at the Market, and one last evening with my family before embarking on our road trip to North Carolina.

We aren't so young, we tell ourselves.

But twenty-four—we are children.

It's mid-August, 1985. In the months ahead, I will think back to this point—everything is new and exciting, and our lives lie before us. We are thrilled to be on our own, with an interval of time to ourselves, undistracted by family and friends.

While I can't imagine what to expect as a "military dependent," I won't be idle—I will start graduate school at the University of North Carolina at Chapel Hill within a month of arriving in Fayetteville. After receiving my acceptance letter from UNC admissions, I glance at a map, but only cursorily; in my pre-wedding euphoria, the dots designating each city look close enough.

Five days after leaving Seattle, we arrive in Fayetteville. It's late—nearly midnight—and raining. The sense of apprehension I've had all day intensifies as we crest the Appalachians and descend into North Carolina's central Piedmont region.

At the city's northern outskirts, a sign greets us: "Welcome to Fayetteville: All American City."

I rouse myself from a restless half-sleep and sit up. As you brake for a stoplight, a slender shape moves sinuously through the linked puddles on the road in front of us.

"What's that?" I demand, suddenly awake.

"Snake," you say. "Creepy."

The creature slithers off the pavement and disappears into the weedy grass of the verge. I shiver. Is this a portent? You glance over at me, guessing my thoughts.

"Don't read too much into it."

We find our new apartment. Neither of us can bear the thought of unloading the car, so we leave everything there.

You start up the staircase in the breezeway between our building and the next, toward our second-floor unit, then abruptly stop short.

"Jesus!" you exclaim as a cigarette end glows hot red, inches in front of you. It illuminates a woman with a taut, wraithlike face who we'll come to know as Cher, sitting on the stairs, smoking in the dark. She regards us with an expressionless, level gaze before expelling a thin stream of smoke over her right shoulder.

"Sorry, didn't see you," you apologize.

She responds only by moving closer to the railing on one side to allow our passage.

The apartment is dark; the power isn't on yet. You start to apologize, but I stop you. We can call the power company in the morning. The narrow beam of the flashlight we keep in the car shows you've taken considerable care to find a nice place, and I'm touched. We fall into bed, exhausted.

The next few days begin to reveal the depth of my youth and inexperience. Three things become clear. First: my complete ignorance of Southern culture. I'd seen most of the Western US, but none of the South. It's like another country entirely. The accent is unfamiliar. I don't know what a hushpuppy is, and have never heard of chiggers or kudzu.

Second: my total lack of experience with the military. This is not just the regular military; Fort Bragg houses a concentration of highly specialized rapid deployment forces—the 82nd Airborne, the Special Forces, Delta Force—known for intensity, stealth, and subterfuge. I learn about the defcon (defense readiness condition) system; above a certain level, you must carry a pager 24/7 and stay near the base. I am warned to be wary of spies preying on vulnerable military dependents.

Third: my naïve assumption that you and I would readily adapt to marriage. *We're newlyweds*, I tell myself. *We're in love.* We're also both willful, stubborn, oldest children who know *we* are *right*, and come from families with very different styles of handling conflict. When you're angry, I know it. In my family, anger didn't exist—only rational, calm discussion. After our first fight, I assume divorce is imminent.

The result: I feel destabilized, a stranger in several strange lands.

The day we spend on base completing my "inprocessing" as a dependent provides abundant evidence that I've waded into wholly unfamiliar waters. It is scorching, nearly 100 degrees, and oppressively humid. Our car, purchased in temperate Seattle, has no air conditioning.

As we travel between drab offices, I gaze out the window, fascinated, my shirt adhering to my back. We pass soldiers running in formation, doing something between singing and chanting:

"I wanna be an Airborne Ranger / Live a life of death and danger…"

You see my puzzled expression and explain: "Running cadence."

I encounter military families for the first time. Many of the wives of enlisted personnel are not yet eighteen, already trailing a string of disheveled and whining children in their wake. I would see them at a few "voluntary-mandatory" family pre-deployment meetings, but never get to know any of them.

The day's highlight is getting my military ID. In the photo, I'm holding a board displaying my dependent ID number, convict-style, with an ironic half-smile. I look hot, tense, and pissed off. When the clerk hands me my freshly laminated card, you immediately reach over my shoulder and pluck it from my hand, then burst into laughter.

"What's so funny?" I demand, retrieving it.

"Your photo. That look says '*Fuck with me and you die.*'"

As five o'clock approaches, we're on our way home. When the south gate comes into view, the cars around us accelerate. You do, too.

"What's the big hurry?" I ask, mystified by this rush to the exit. You start to answer:

"If you're on-post at five..."

Your words are drowned out by the tinny and distorted but unmistakable strains of "Taps," blaring from speakers affixed to the telephone poles lining the road. All the cars skid to a dusty stop, including ours. Soldiers leap from them and stand at attention next to open car doors, right hands raised in stiff salutes.

Life off-post is equally bizarre. One afternoon, I present my new military ID to a clerk at the neighborhood video store. She looks at it, glances at my application, and returns it.

"Sorry, miss. One account per family."

I'm confused, which she interprets as abject stupidity.

"On your application, *here*," she says, stabbing impatiently at the form with scarlet nails so long they spiral at the ends, "There's one name. On your ID, *here*, another. One family, one account. Two families, two accounts. Store policy—see here?" She taps a crudely handwritten notice taped to the counter. "Really," she adds, shaking her head sadly, "It ain't so hard."

I finally understand. "I get it. I was just married, but didn't change my name." I extend my ID again. "See? That's my husband's last name, and there's mine. They're different, but it says I'm his wife. One account, one family, two names."

The clerk looks flummoxed. Shaking her head with an expression blending irritation and pity, she asks:

"Why...why, *honey*, don't you *like* his name?"

She pronounces "like" with elaborate disdain: *laaaaahhhke*.

Our second week in Fayetteville, I'm scheduled to enroll for fall semester at Chapel Hill. Since leaving Seattle, I've given little thought to the start of the school year, and haven't again consulted a map.

The night before that first trip north, you suggest I look at a map and write out directions so I won't be tempted to try to read it while driving.

"Good idea," I agree, before returning to the book I'm reading. I'm in no hurry. My appointment isn't until one o'clock.

The next morning, I unfold the map on the counter and study it over coffee. I find Fayetteville and Chapel Hill, measure the distance between them, then consult the legend showing the scale. I frown.

That can't be right, I think, and repeat these steps. A sense of deep unease begins in my chest and quickly expands into full-scale dread.

Chapel Hill is 90 miles northeast of Fayetteville. The most direct route is north on Highway 87 to Sanford, then northeast on Highway 501. Both are small, two-lane state highways.

My heart sinks. *Ninety* miles, *one* way! Three hours' round trip, at least. I panic. I can't possibly do that daily. My worst fears will be realized. I'll have to drop out of graduate school. I'll end up flipping burgers for the next three years at the local Hardee's. My mind will rot. I'll get pregnant, forcing you to stay in the military to support a family. We'll spend twenty years trailing from base to base, military nomads. My parents will be appalled. They'll never say "We told you so," but they won't need to.

I can't let down my parents, or you. Or me. So I go. My first semester is terrifying. Aside from the long drive, I dislike my classes—in grammar, research methods, and Romantic literature, the last taught by an aging professor who sees phallic references everywhere and loves "poims." In the campus's central square, I watch a running battle between vitriolic evangelists who warn students about the hellfire awaiting those who don't accept "*Jay*sus," and the students who heckle them mercilessly in return. I leave campus every day after classes, so I know no one.

The single scrap of good news is that I manage to arrange a schedule with all Tuesday-Thursday classes, making the commute tolerable. But my pervasive fear of failure continues unchecked, and I fret for the better part of each 90-mile trip.

In Fayetteville, things go from strange to stranger.

I'm awakened one night by the phone's insistent ringing. You're impervious and continue snoring. I get out of bed; it's 2:20 a.m. *Who's calling at this hour?*

I stumble to the hallway and answer it. After a pause, I hear a terse male voice:

"This Sullie's wife? Need to talk with him. Right away, please."

Sullie? My half-awake brain doesn't immediately recognize this as your nickname.

"Oh…Kevin," I say after a moment's hesitation.

I awaken you and you take the call. When you hang up, you tell me your unit has been called out and you must be at your garrison within the hour. You hurriedly dress and gather your pre-packed gear. As we drive toward Bragg, I ask questions: Going where? How long? An exercise or the real thing? You have no answers, but assure me I should hear from the "wives' telephone network" tomorrow. Outside your garrison, you kiss me through the open car window, sling your gear over your shoulder, and melt into a sea of olive drab. I return alone to a silent apartment.

The next afternoon, a woman calls to tell me in a laconic Midwestern accent that your unit completed a predawn training jump into Fort Benning, Georgia, and is on a field exercise. You'll return "in a few days."

You're home within the week. Until then, I'm desperately, achingly lonely. I know no one in Fayetteville and still barely know my fellow students. I was never homesick while an undergraduate in California so hadn't expected this overwhelming loneliness.

When your unit travels to Panama that fall for a month's "jungle training," I miss you fiercely and feel utterly alone. I begin to worry about my state of mind one afternoon when sitting in our bedroom, trying to read through a deep haze of loneliness. I dread the weekend ahead, with nothing planned, no one to see. Despite the heat, I open the windows so I can hear the cicadas whirring and buzzing outside and smell the sharp fragrance of the pines.

When the air thickens with moisture and a distant rumble announces an approaching storm, I move to the window. Southern thunderstorms fascinate me. As the first white flash of lightning illuminates the darkened room and the answering thunder rolls across the sky, I glance back over my shoulder.

A table lamp sits on the dresser, its turquoise ceramic base shaped like a ginger jar. As I watch, it slowly levitates, hangs suspended in the air, then floats toward the door. I blink and look again; surely I'm imagining it. But the lamp's still there, hovering. *That's it*, I think to myself, *I'm hallucinating. Losing my mind.* I call my mother, panicked and weeping. My worried father arranges for me to spend the weekend with his aunt and uncle in Charlotte. I'm immensely grateful for their warm welcome.

Gradually, I gain confidence and shed my assumption of failure. My classes become tolerable. I start to regain my balance. I find myself anticipating favorite sections on my commute to school—the bridge spanning the Haw River, the deciduous forest northeast of Sanford, which glows yellow and burnished gold at the height of autumn before the leaves fall, leaving a lacy canopy of silver branches. Pittsboro, with its eighteenth-century City Hall at the center of town. And just outside Chapel Hill, the pastoral fields of Fearrington, where I always look for the herd of belted Galloway cattle.

I finish my first semester with respectable grades, and we celebrate my perseverance. We celebrate Christmas, too, making an enormous dinner with new neighbors downstairs that we share with two Privates from your unit, far from their homes with nowhere to go. I'm increasingly aware of this time's value—away from everything familiar, learning to be married without an audience of family and friends. We make mistakes, but slowly learn to mend them and move on.

Early the next spring, I'm driving to Chapel Hill at dawn on a Monday morning. The road is practically empty; it's too early for the lumbering, rural-route school buses or the chicken trucks showering white feathers behind them. I watch the eastern sky brighten as the sun rises, modulating from golden yellow to shades of pink and orange. I inhale deeply; the lush humidity carries with it the fragrance of honeysuckle. I'm surprised to catch myself thinking, *I love this drive.*

My second semester at Chapel Hill brings better classes and new friends. Spring in North Carolina is breathtakingly beautiful. In the deciduous forests, the warming air coaxes forth the blossoms of the redbud and dogwood trees, creating misty patches of deep pink and starry white among the still-bare branches.

This semester, I travel to Chapel Hill three times a week. The drive offers more than scenery. One day, I pass a chain gang working in a field. Ten men labor in leg irons while a guard stands watch nearby, a rifle held in the crook of his arm, his right foot resting on a field stone. When I see them ahead, I slow reflexively, at once fascinated and repelled. A few turn to look at me as I pass, their expressions unreadable.

They're there for three days. By the third day, I recognize a few faces. It turns out they've been watching me, too. As I approach the group and slow a little, one of the prisoners, a tall black man, rests his hoe against a fencepost and raises his right hand in a somber greeting. Surprised, I raise my travel coffee mug in return. *Top of the morning to you.* In my rear view mirror, I see him gazing after me.

Slowly, you and I begin to see the richness surrounding us. The South is a wonderful, weird place, and so much is new and unexpected. Still, we spend the balance of our time in Fayetteville eagerly anticipating the day we leave the city.

In the fall of 1987, you're granted an "early out." Your active duty will end in February, 1988. I graduate that December.

Two weeks before our departure, I drop you off at your garrison and spend the morning in our apartment, packing. I'm surprised to find myself feeling melancholy—why? After lunch, I drive to a park on the Cape Fear River. I walk on a winding trail that follows the riverbank. It's quiet and serene, and the woods are bathed in diffuse, golden afternoon light.

As I pass a stand of Southern Pine, I stop, my gaze arrested. Clinging to the rough bark of a pine trunk is an enormous celadon-green moth, its wingspan nearly six inches.

Luna. I've seen photos of this amazing insect, but never imagined seeing one in its natural setting. Its wings are the color of the sea. Elegant tails descend from the lower wings, while dark spots like kohl-rimmed eyes peer from all four. I'm captivated.

Moving closer, I see the moth's elaborate antennae, tightly curled like the decorative scroll on a violin's neck. The crushed velvet texture of its wings draws my hand involuntarily and my fingertip brushes a wing's edge. The Luna flutters off the tree and lands on my bare left arm, where it resumes its languid fanning. I stand frozen, barely able to resist flinching at the *scritch scritch* of the moth's feet on my skin. A minute passes.

Abruptly, the Luna launches off my arm and ascends in a helix-like spiral, soon melting into the canopy above.

Standing there, I realize the source of my melancholy: I'm reluctant to leave North Carolina. It has been the stage—the crucible—for the first years of our marriage. We still would face difficulties ahead; things never would become easy. But our time in Fayetteville—and my trips to Chapel Hill—had provided a unique setting and magical space for these earliest days. Here is where our journey begins.

We Came Over on the Mayflower
By Eve M. Tai

STRANGERS CLUTTERED MY CHILDHOOD. One by one, foreigners boarded Pan Am jumbo jets in Taiwan and flew across the Pacific to America. And one by one, my parents ushered them into our suburban Detroit home. These newcomers, I was told, were our aunts, third uncles and second cousins. Our relatives.

Our relatives carried woven plastic bags thick with blankets and coats, embroidered slippers and soft cover books in Chinese. They set up camp in our guestroom with the double bed smothered in a polyester floral bedspread. The bedroom overlooked a treeless backyard, which merged into the treeless backyards of our neighbors. It was the bedroom I wanted, but could never have.

Our guest bedroom rarely stood empty. Across the hall, I shared a room papered in petunias with my younger sister. More than anything, I wanted a room of my own. I wanted respite from my sister's stuffed animal zoo and her tight-lipped glares whenever I sang along to an Eagles song on the radio. I was tired of negotiating whose twin bed would go where or whose bulletin board would fit best in the space between the windows. The only agreement we could reach was to line our beds and desks up in perfect symmetry in order to be "fair," an arrangement that left me feeling like we were living inside of a mirror.

My Aunt Brenda was the first to arrive. I was almost ten years old when she left Taiwan in 1970 to live with us. She wore plaid capris and cardigans and clipped bobby pins in her hair. Every day she attended classes at the same university where my father taught. Aunt Brenda studied business school texts at my little desk, a Chinese-English dictionary to the side. Sometimes my father tried to soothe her homesickness by showing slides from his Kodak carousel marked "Taiwan, 1968." But she would only sob in to her pillow later that night.

Third Great Uncle came next. He was my father's favorite uncle, and my sister, brother and I loved him too. He spoke with kindness and ease and gave us little red and gold tins of Tiger Balm. A few years later my mother's baby brother and his fiancée arrived. Raised in Taiwan's tropical climate, they were stunned to experience their first blizzard. And then came my grandmother, who joined the rotation for months at a time, chainsaw snoring through the night.

"I need my own room," I announced to my parents one night as we retired to the family room after dinner. I was twelve. "I need my privacy."

"*Mei Mei*," my mother sighed, addressing me as "little sister." The effect was affectionate and patronizing at the same time.

"Privacy?" my father snorted. "There's no such word in Chinese."

"No one in China has her own room," my mother said. Trumped again by China. It was always China this, China that. When would my parents realize that we lived in Michigan?

Defeated, I skulked off to my shared bedroom and indulged in fantasy. I pictured transforming the guestroom into my private suite. I lay on the floor with a stack of old computer paper from my mother's chemistry lab and began to draw various layouts. I cut out decorating ideas from *Seventeen* magazine -- a frothy seafoam bedspread and a princess telephone on a nightstand. But with every new arrival from Taiwan, the chances of winning my own bedroom dwindled from slim to none.

Not only did our relatives occupy the coveted guestroom, they carried a *carte blanche* pass that gained them exclusive access to my parents. They spoke in ciphered language about events, places and people unknown to me – Shanghai streets, sweet potatoes, shadowy military officers. It was like watching a foreign spy movie without subtitles and trying to follow the plot and the characters. I could speak Chinese and I still couldn't unravel the code shared between my relatives and my parents.

"It's mango season in Taiwan," an auntie would say. "Remember how wonderful they smelled in the market?" My mother would nod, her face sober. Back then hydroponic tomatoes and tasteless Delicious apples populated American supermarket produce bins. Nobody had ever heard of a mango.

Sometimes my parents and relatives' voices would drop to a whisper, especially about *tao nan*. *Tao nan,* I later learned from an Amy Tan novel, was the panicked exodus of Chinese after the Communists won the civil war and assumed power in Beijing. Both of my parents' families had been allied with the opposition and were forced to flee to Taiwan.

My parents themselves had migrated to America only a few years before my birth. My mother, I often noticed, would avoid eye contact with the gas station attendant and the grocery store clerk, casting her gaze down at the floor. Sometimes my parents would even speak broken English, a phenomenon that bewildered me because both were fluent speakers. My parents were both professors and American citizens. Yet the presence of "real" Americans seemed to trigger in them a backcountry demeanor. "We're outsiders," I once heard my father say to a cousin as they brewed tea in our kitchen. "We have to be careful."

If my parents felt displaced in America, my relatives made me feel displaced in my own home. I often complained that we were running a free hotel where the guests' well-being superseded mine. I was supposed to be cheerful about it too.

"Do you know how hard it is to be so far from home?" my mother would ask me in that this-is-not-really-a-question kind of way. My parents took offense whenever I referred to our relatives as "them," or especially as "strangers." I couldn't seem to explain that our relatives were, in fact, people I didn't know.

Each time a new aunt or uncle arrived, my parents would roll out more pork dumplings and add more jasmine rice to the rice cooker. While I had to beg for a new board game and was told to save my allowance because "we're not rich," my relatives ate and drank and bathed and talked on the phone without one peep from my father about a "budget."

Although just a girl, compared to our relatives I felt savvy and worldly, simply because I was American. I knew how to order hamburgers at Big Boy, how to get to Chatham's supermarket on the corner of Eleven Mile and Middlebelt, how to read the *Detroit News*. I'd visited the Great Smoky Mountains, Disney World and Chicago. I could read the exhibit signs at the Greenfield Village Museum that chronicled the rise of American industry and the stories of Henry Ford, Thomas Edison and Charles Goodyear.

My parents frequently asked me to accompany our relatives on tours of the Ford Motor Company to observe the auto assembly lines and fiery steel pits. My relatives would listen to the tour guide patiently and then ask me what she had said. Though my Chinese was hardly mature enough to explain that Ford was the only car company that manufactured their own steel with iron ore shipped by barge over the Great Lakes, their questions made me feel sophisticated.

I viewed our various family members the way I might have regarded new kids at school. They were newcomers, with odd mannerisms and awkward questions at the mall about which was the men's bathroom and which was the women's. Our relatives wore socks with sandals, mixed pungent powders into their tea mugs and stared at me curiously as though I were a lab specimen, the result of crossing Chinese heritage with an American upbringing.

The Americanized Chinese Girl. It was something to guard against. My parents weren't happy with my affinity for watching *Three's Company* or cavorting in the woods near our house building forts and playing pioneers. Sometimes I'd even play the other side, the Indians. I'd braid my hair and wear a rose suede vest with fur tassels that my parents had bought for me in the Wisconsin Dells. Then I'd switch back to the Pilgrims and cut out paper buckles and paste them to my shoes.

"*We* came over on the Mayflower," I told my mother once. "*We* ate turkey with the Indians. They were savages until *we* made friends with them."

I knew of course, that Miles Standish and the lot of them weren't my blood ancestors. But I wanted that heritage for my own because it made me feel more American. Though I may have been born in the same Michigan hospital as my schoolmates, my relatives' constant presence marked me as an outsider too. So my goal was to become the average American family, or at least the average American girl. We would be just like our neighbors, everyday families with mom and dad and the kids, a station wagon and a Golden Retriever.

We fought the Indians. *We* fought the Redcoats. I always included myself on the "we" side.

In my mid-twenties I visited the Southwest for the first time with my parents. Usually I vacationed up north around Traverse City, where pine and maple forests met up with the green-blue expanse of Lake Michigan. In New Mexico though, everything was colored from the Earth's palette—orange, flame-red, sienna.

It was spring. The light shone on and on over sandy floors and canyons. Everywhere you looked there was that sky, as though Lake Michigan had been tossed up into the heavens. There was a stillness and peace that the Southwest almost demanded, and I began to understand how Native Americans had developed such a close kinship to this landscape. I felt it too. It warmed me and gave me the willies all at once.

My mother and I visited a museum in Albuquerque where we found early portraits of Apache and Navajo tribal members. In a flash, a memory from fifth grade seized me. A wrinkled substitute teacher. A gray autumn morning. The teacher's equally gray hair tied up in a bun. She asked us what we were studying.

"Thanksgiving," a boy said.

"Yeah, with the Pilgrims and Indians," another boy said.

"Thanksgiving?" the substitute said. I was shocked to see her actually sneer. "You know what that story is?" she hissed. She leaned forward over the wooden desk.

My classmates and I shrank back in our seats.

"Bunk!" The teacher pounded her fist on the desk. "The white man came over here from Europe"—she was almost snarling now—"and he killed every Indian man, woman and baby he could find and took away everything they had."

I glanced at our construction paper turkeys, traced from the shapes of our hands and taped to the classroom windows. Our teacher was right, of course. We may have only been in fifth grade and frightened, but we knew the truth when we heard it, even if we couldn't admit it.

I would never learn about Native American tribes in my school lessons on pioneer history. I suppose our young minds were to assume that the rest of the country was chock full of forests, rivers and prairies, devoid of people until settlers pushed west. I didn't learn about the slaughter of tribes, of the equally tragic slaughter of great herds of bison -- one of the most sacred animals to Native Americans -- sacrificed not for food, clothing or shelter, but for sport.

Back in the Albuquerque museum, I studied the faces in the portrait gallery. I soaked in their dress—their feathers, beads and face paint. Each man, woman and child carried a story that I would never hear. The black and white pictures haunted me, not only because those cultures had been decimated, but also because looking into their eyes was like facing our own damaged history. Of facing ourselves.

But for me, the idea of looking into a reflection was more than just a metaphor. When I looked into those faces I saw my own forebears. I saw myself.

So many millennia after crossing the land bridge in Alaska, the faces of those first Americans still looked Asian. Chinese, even. Standing in the light of a New Mexico day I saw our connection so clearly. We shared the same curve over our eye sockets, the same eyes shaped like minnows, the same black hair, the same broad cheekbones. We looked alike. I shivered, as though these men, women and children, long gone, were passing their spirits through me. These photographs all told me the simple truth—these were people whose blood I shared. These were my relatives.

Relatives. By then, I hadn't thought about our Chinese relatives and their early days in America for years, perhaps a decade or more. They'd all eventually moved out of our guestroom and found jobs, mates and homes. My Aunt Brenda, the one who had cried into her pillow at night, was now a married mother of two living in Canada. Every Christmas she sent pastel-colored acrylic sweaters and Nissan steel hotpots. Her children spoke Chinese, English and French. My mother's baby brother and his wife fled snowy Michigan and moved to Los Angeles where they were raising two daughters. My aunt was now selling multi-million dollar properties to clients whom she chauffeured in her Mercedes.

My relatives' adjustment had erased my memories of their awkward transition, that time when they used to stumble over words like "throw," and say "srow" instead. They still mispronounced their words, but I had stopped caring long ago. My once fervent wish that my family would become more American had been granted and I hadn't even noticed.

Perhaps this was because I had begun to find my own way, out of my parents' house and hold certainly, but in my life as well. When I graduated from college I moved with job in hand to Chicago. It was the perfect place for me. It gave me the big city energy I craved and comforted me with its Midwestern sensibility.

As the years had passed, visits from my relatives had gradually waned. I came home once from Chicago on a non-holiday, startled to find no one save for my parents. Gone was the bustle in the kitchen, of gossiping and roasted watermelon seeds cracked between molars as the teakettle whistled. The only sound in the kitchen now came from the refrigerator compressor cycling on and off.

The Native American portraits showed me how I had withheld from my own relatives the empathy I felt for the first Americans. The courage required of my relatives to immigrate to a new country of snow, sneers and super highways had not differed much from the courage it had taken those first Americans to traverse canyons full of mountain lions, swift waters and poisonous berries.

My mother stood next to me in the gallery and studied another portrait. I saw the same spirit pass through her that had shifted through me only a moment before. When our eyes met, I could see that we both no longer believed that she and my father and our relatives were newcomers. Now we knew that our forebears had forged this territory called America long, long before the Mayflower.

We had been here all along.

Father, Complex

By Natalie Singer

Once, on a steamy Florida evening as I lay in bed in my cotton nightgown, I caught sight of my father as he sat outside on my swing, cigarette smoke rising in the pale dusk. His head bobbed up and down, the way it did when he listened to his Beach Boys records. I crept to my bedroom window.

The blue-and-white metal swing set, aglow in the early night, was my favorite thing: I spent hours on its slide and seats and bars. I hated to leave it when my mother called me in for dinner; often I would long for it through the night, dreaming of its cool poles and rocking motions.

"Nou?" My father called me softly by my nickname, like a question. He lifted me carefully through the open window and into the yard. My mom, probably washing dishes, would never have let me out so late. The blades of grass swept my feet, and I could smell the ocean in the air. My curly hair, thick and moist and too heavy for a four-year-old's head, must have frizzed a little extra at the wall of heat outside. The fat frogs that suctioned to the side of our stucco on hot nights burped their low croaks. My dad's face was lobster red, the flush of my parents' sun-worship. It radiated against his dark curls and white Lacoste T-shirt, tight against his lanky, twenty-nine-year-old frame.

He lowered me onto the swing and pulled me back, then released. I pumped my skinny legs higher against the darkening sky and watched the twinkling stars slide out from behind the swirls of my dad's smoke.

***

I was 15 the last time in my childhood that we spoke. We sat in his car on a windy night, parked outside what would soon no longer be my house. We were moving away—not my father, but me and my brother and my mother, along with her new husband and his kids. Brady Bunch-like, we were headed to California, across the continent, to follow my stepfather's job. My father was the sole member of our original family unit being left behind.

I was still a child, but he spoke to me in a stiff voice as though I was an adult. Boardroom voice, I thought of it secretly, the voice of business deals. Or like an angry man speaks to an errant wife.

"Do you want to go?" he demanded.

"I don't know," I countered. "It's a good opportunity." Repeating the mantra I had been told a million times already by my mother and stepfather.

"I'm going to fight your mother taking your brother."

"You can't do that! Please, don't do that, Dad. You can't separate us … " I trailed off. Steam spread across the windows.

"Oh yeah? Well who's thinking of me? Damn it, what about what I'm losing?" He slammed the steering wheel. I remember wondering if it shouldn't be my mother out there in the car, putting up defenses. The wife who cheated on him and left, instead of the teen-age daughter who just looked and sounded a lot like her.

In the subdivision of families, there are tiny heartbreaks everywhere.

The car fight was the last salvo in a battle that had been building since my parents divorced a few years earlier. Our disappointments piled up quickly. After the divorce he became a weekend father, most of our time spent awkwardly in pizza joints and movie theaters. He dated and soon married a woman who I thought held me in contempt, clicking her tongue at my wiry hair and offering me "makeovers" every time I arrived from my mother's house. There was no space for me in their home or on their vacations; every molecule of energy was sucked up by her tantrumming preschooler. My brother, five years younger than me, was more easily absorbed.

And I had attitude. Adult complexities could not translate to me: In my adolescent vernacular, divorce was just a synonym for failure. So I pulled away, too, hung up the phone on the booming boardroom voice.

Maybe I erased myself from this melancholy family tableau in order to save myself—a rescue operation only a fresh-mouthed teen-age girl could carry off. But I suppose it doesn't really matter who was at fault. In the end none of us fought very hard. There was never counseling, no heartfelt pleas for family unity. Just a slow falling away, until contact between my father and I, and everyone on his side of the family, ceased.

***

Life carried on, distractions presented themselves. Soon after the silence began, I drew into my sights a target for my budding teen-age girl obsessions.

Loren was twenty, and he was my camp counselor. That summer my fifteen-year-old friends and I were assigned to a special, remote section of our camp in a program called "Pioneers," meant to teach us skills for self-reliance. In reality that meant a bunch of horny teenagers, half of them pretty girls, being supervised day and night by a handful of college kids, half of them man-boys like Loren.

I was taken with him from the day we piled off the school bus that ferried us from the suburban mall parking lot up into the mountains. Compared to the boys at school—boys my age who were either juvenile or stupid or popular enough to be dismissive of me—Loren was another species. He could pitch a tent, cook a meal over a fire, had his driver's license and spent his days off back in the city hanging out at the college bars.

He listened when I spoke. I could talk with him about books and ideas and the flaws of our parents. That summer and in the months that followed, I would confide in Loren about my family, during a short window when the disappointments were still fresh and anger hadn't rooted deeply enough to quiet me.

He was kind, funny and had a sexy-goofy smile that made me feel fluttery on the inside in a way I never had before. Long after curfew, I would sneak out of my bunk, tiptoe across the shadows of the mess hall and pine trees, and slip through the front flap of Loren's platform tent. He always seemed to be waiting for me, listening to his Discman and burning incense to hide the smell of his cigarettes. He let me watch him smoke but rarely allowed me a drag.

The platform tents were freezing in the mountain nights. I wriggled my way into his warm bed, anything to get close to him. He let me cuddle up in a sisterly way. But he always stopped me when I tried to engage him, which I did time and time again with a silly 15-year-old giggle and pout. I had discovered lust, and he was killing me with his resistance. Making out with Loren—and whatever came after making out, which I wasn't fully certain of but fairly desperate to discover— was all I thought about that summer and the better part of the year that followed, during which we stayed friends.

With a look or a wink, Loren let me know I affected him. But his answer was the same every time I threw myself down into his lap, made a suggestive comment, or voiced impatience with my fast-waning childhood.

"You're too young," he would say, looking seriously at me. "You shouldn't be in such a hurry. All of it is going to happen for you, Natalie. Just take your time."

There was nothing wrong with him. He was good looking, tall and slender and dark, which I was beginning to understand was my type. I knew he was intimate with older girls. But he wouldn't lay a hand on me, even in the most compromised situations. At a friend's house once during the following winter he and I went into a closet alone and I climbed on top of him in a straddle, enjoying the intoxicating moment of newly discovered feminine power only long enough for him to shake his head with a smile and firmly lift me off.

He promised me when I turned eighteen, if it was right, he might be different with me. But long before I could hold him to it, I was gone. I left on an airplane for a new California life with nothing more than a chaste kiss on the mouth that I bullied him into at the end of our goodbye.

I tried always to take Loren's kindly rejection with a brave face, to let it slide off my new, tough veneer. I was never angry at him; I knew how good he was. But inside I hid my few minutes of broken hearted-ness. He was, he will always be, my first love.

***

By the time I am twenty-two, I haven't spoken to my father for nearly eight years.

It is my senior year of college, and I still live at home with my mother in the suburbs outside San Francisco. For several years I have been dating the dull and sexually lackluster Jim, a police-officer-in-training with whom I fake orgasms and reluctantly eat dinner with at the local TGI Fridays.

I spend hours a day commuting to my college classes in San Francisco by car or train and wake at five a.m. to sling espresso at Starbucks before school. I have few friends. I am dragged down by the commute, my overfull schedule and by the endless floating fog and gray mist that shroud the campus. Sometimes I feel lost, momentarily confused about where it is I am walking to as I cross the wet quad, unable to remember which classes I am taking or what material I studied or why I am even here.

I am itchy in my routine, bored to pieces, hungry for the "real" life to start. I speak to no one about my fog and the panic that seems to follow me everywhere. My family assumes I am fine, on track with my classes and planning a career. No one thinks to ask me what my days are like. I don't think to explain them.

In the fall I land an internship at an independent newspaper in the city. On my first day I walk in and meet the young editor of the paper. I fall in love (lust?) on the spot.

Zev is thirty-three. His parents came from Croatia; he lives with them in his house in San Francisco's Sunset District. He drives a Volkswagen. He loves baseball in a sweetly passionate way (I learn quickly that we will all cover for him when the Giants have a big game). He wears Vans sneakers and has thick black hair and is so adult and so incredibly sexy that sometimes, as I sit at my desk doing intern busywork, I almost cry in frustration at how badly I want him. At home in bed at night I do cry.

During my shifts I sit and stare at his back, his head bent over his desk, his lips moving into the phone. He is my boss in the most direct sense—I am his editorial assistant—and this means I receive my tasks from him. This heightens the sexually charged younger-woman-older-man dynamic. I am his assistant! This involves me going into his tiny office, something that causes me to sweat and hyperventilate and fantasize incessantly. He always invites me to sit. He gives me plum reporting assignments when I should be doing calendar entries. He favors my work. After six months he offers me a full-time job. "You *have* to come work for me," he says, staring at me from underneath his dark eyebrows.

For the first half of the year, Zev is single. His girlfriend has left him. This is my window: I could ask to buy him a drink after work under the auspices of mentorly advice. This is my chance to be a grown woman, to offer myself to Zev the way I had with Loren. In my mind Zev and I are so perfect for each other that not only will we have incredible, orgasm-inducing sex but we will sit in our sunny breakfast nook looking out over the sparkling bay and read *The New York Times* on Sundays together. I want to do everything to him. I want him to do anything to me.

One winter night, Zev walks me out to my car, parked around a corner in the gang-ridden Western Addition neighborhood where the paper's shoddy offices are housed. The air is damp; I shiver in my wool coat. Police sirens wail down a nearby street.

"How's school going?" he asks, kicking a rock with his navy Vans.

This is your chance, ask him you loser.

"It's fine," I say. "It's a lot of work. I can't wait to be done."

"Are you going to come work for me?"

"I'd love to talk about it some time," I stammer, even though I know it's unlikely. I want to go work for a bigger newspaper, get out of town when I graduate. Unless. Unless Zev and I are together. Then, I would stay.

Now. Let's talk now. Over beer. Speak.

But I can't. I am paralyzed. Terrified. Why am I so scared? Why don't I think I'm good enough for this smart, beautiful man?

"Well, here you go," he says, handing me some back issues of the paper I am lugging home in a stack. I fumble for my keys, and he watches me get into my car before spinning back into the darkness.

The second half of the year slams the door shut: Zev's worried Old Country parents import a Croatian "family friend" whom Zev knocks up and marries in a hurry. My internship finishes in the spring. I never see him again.

***

When the silence between my father and I began, I was a child. By my college graduation, the transformation was long since complete; I had gone from relative innocent to sexual being.

What does this mean, that my maturation took place away from his supervision? That he had no knowledge of, bore no witness to, the development of my sexual identity? Maybe nothing. But my new stepfamily soon fell apart, and the grown-ups left in my life were distracted. By seventeen, I was under my own authority, carefully cultivating a stubborn self-sufficiency that became central to my personality—the consummate Pioneer.

There was no fatherly advice to steer me through the temptations of high school or the isolation of college. Instead, I parented myself closely. Mostly, I maintained tight control. When I did not, my well-being was left to the ethics of others, or to the odds of fate.

When I step across the stage in a shiny purple cap and gown to accept my university diploma, my father is sitting in the audience alongside my mother, beaming. His hair is graying. He seems shorter than eight years ago. I don't know how he came to be here on this sunny day in May – did one of us take a stand, demand finally an end to it? I think no. Like the first slow falling away, our relationship somehow underwent a quiet knitting back together, like cells programmed to regenerate at the site of a wound.

After the ceremony, he helps me pack my suburban bedroom into U-Haul boxes and advises me on my contract negotiations with the southern California newspaper that has hired me. He writes checks for a couch and groceries and buys me extra locks for my new apartment's rickety sliding-glass door.

"There are crazy people in the world," he reminds me more than once over the phone, after I've driven down the coast to my new life. "Did you install those locks yet? We have to make sure you're safe."

Over the next decade, he calls me every weekend, no matter where I live, no matter if one of us is traveling, or sick, or distracted. He never misses a call. We don't speak of the time in between, never say to each other I'm sorry … I should have … What happened to you? Did you turn out OK, you know, on the inside?

At first I think about posing these questions pointedly during a phone call, or over one of the seafood dinners he treats me to when he's in town.

But I never do, and soon I stop thinking about them.

Two years after we begin speaking, my father stands beside me at my wedding, to a tall, sandy-haired writer five years my senior who reads me poetry in bed and does my laundry when I let it go too long.

Now my father sends us airplane tickets to come visit him, and when he visits us for holidays and after the birth of each baby, he tells us how proud he is. Often he comments about what a good man and father my husband is.

"He's a good boy, that Lukas," my father says often.

He is right. My husband fathers our young daughters lovingly, takes them to the park and ballet lessons and throws them over his shoulder like an ogre before bed. He winces as if pained when he is forced to think about them growing up—dates, driving lessons, college applications. He makes funny proclamations like, "Not until you're twenty-five!"

But I have a feeling it will pass more quickly than we know. In my mind's eye I can picture him, waiting up in our armchair for the key in the door, double-checking the locks on their windows. Cupping their first heartaches carefully in his hand.

The Urban Goatherd

By Elizabeth Corcoran Murray

September, 1980

It takes me three days to hitchhike from Paris to St. Pons. I hop from a muddy Renault into a patch of Monet red poppies. I smell wild thyme from the mountains as my ride grinds its gears and disappears around the curve. The pencil-drawn map from my pocket is withered and frayed. "Look for a small cross beside the road," it reads, "then a clearing, and finally a trail." A voice from the trees startles me.

"Elizabeth?" Elton's smile broadens in surprise. "My cousin!" he jests, for we are third cousins, barely cousins at all. "I wasn't expecting you!" We hike to his *petit* stone house, wreathed with white roses, hidden in the forest. We huddle before the fire, sip chamomile tea in the darkness. Finally he asks, "What are you doing here?" I've been wondering the same thing.

I perch on a short stool, my knees up to my chin. The fire spits saffron flames. I wrap his blanket around my shoulders. "Greg was the love of my life." My fingers trace the curves of the cup's chipped rim. "Here I am, twenty-six, and Greg was my first love." I look up at Elton. "It worked for a while, and then it didn't," I say. "I needed to go. Anywhere. I decided to backpack around Europe. First, I visited my college roommate in London, then a childhood friend in Paris, and now I'm here. I had saved this little map you drew the last time we met, almost two years ago."

During the next steaming September days, Elton and I yank weeds that flourish between the leeks and lettuce in his garden. "Elizabeth," he says. "My friend from the neighboring village is hiring a goatherd. Would you like the job?"

"Like in *The Sound of Music*?" I imagine the enchanted life of the lonely goatherd, singing in the Alps. I grew up in Holyoke, Massachusetts, an industrial city. I have never been on a farm, and barely recognize a goat from a sheep. "What's a goatherd do?"

"Well, she ensures the goats are safe and eat well. The females are for milking and the male goats are used for their meat. The goatherd leads the animals to trees and bushes where they'll graze, and then they shift to other spots throughout the day."

"I'm a city person." I say. "You know. Indoors. Sedentary." But maybe this will be like Outward Bound, I muse, where people pay for wilderness experiences. Or maybe I'll write a book. I don't know how long I'll stay or what I'll get paid, but "yes," I say. "Yes, I'll be a goatherd."

"No one in the family speaks English," Elton warns me. I barely speak French.

A few days later, I hitchhike to the town square where I'm to meet Camille Fontaine, my new employer. I spy a woman with a sun-sized smile and tortoise-shell glasses waving across the dusty market. She kisses me on each cheek, and throws my backpack in her tin car. Camille, I presume. We drive past fields speckled with fragrant thyme and crumbling ruins, until, an hour later, we arrive at a village of only four homes.

Camille thrusts open the thick wood door, where the spicy aroma of leek soup greets us. I freeze, gaping at the bare cement floor, stone walls, two rectangular tables, wood cooking stove, pile of buckets, ladder leading to the lofts, and the tiny window carved into eight-inch-thick walls. This two-hundred-year-old home has no heat, no plumbing, and only two bare light bulbs.

Camille beckons me up first one ladder to an attic, then a second ladder to a loft barely large enough to contain the mattress I will share with the teenage daughter for the next seven months. Climbing back down, it's time for work. Camille flips her shiny hair as she ties her shoulder-to-hip apron. My job is to peel potatoes. I curl my hair around my ear, feeling relieved. Something familiar. I can peel, certainly. The scent of firewood wafts through the kitchen, as she hands me a knife, peels part of a potato, then tosses it to me. Camille throws wood on the fire, washes some pots, comes back to me. I can do this, I think. Then I look more closely. There are at least thirty potatoes. The knife is dull. Camille takes a spud back from me.

"*Vite! Vite!*" she says. Hurry up! She demonstrates, peeling the potato in seconds. I pick up my pace and eventually peel the stack. "Now, cut," she apparently says. Once again she models for me. Zip! Zip! Her knife slams through the potato, drums against the table. Her potato is sliced. For me: zip, zip, zip, and about eight more zips, I have the second one sliced. Camille scowls under her auburn bangs. Her smile vanishes as the evening sun slips behind the mountains.

The Fontaines and I assemble on benches to eat our supper in the *salle de manger*, where a fireplace extends from one end of the room to the other. A black cauldron, reminiscent of Macbeth, dangles over the embers.

After our meal, Camille gestures me outside to a vehicle that looks like a miniature oil truck. It supplies our water. Camille takes the attached hose and fills two buckets. She carts them into the *salle de manger* to pour into the cauldron. We boil the water to wash the dishes. I fill my two pails, then tug on the metal handles. They slice my palms. Water sloshes over my shoes. I feel like I'm heaving boulders from the ancient ruins. I rest a minute, listening to goats' bells tinkle in the nearby barn. I pull, futilely, on the pails again. Finally, I grab one bucket at a time with two hands and waddle to the table inside. My legs and shoes are drenched. Camille frowns. Between peeling potatoes and carrying water, I get an "F" for my first day on the farm.

I lie awake upstairs next to Camille's snoring daughter, fixing my eyes on the rafters inches from my face. I'm discouraged, yet something in the air, the mountains, the simple lifestyle, calls to me. I hear the goats sing their soft sounds as I drift to sleep.

The scent of chicory and coffee wakes me. I stumble down the ladder and pour myself a hot drink. Jacques, Camille's husband, stands in the doorway, his feet planted like John Wayne. He wears grey, baggy pants, tied at the waist with a rope. "It's time to take the goats out," he seems to say in his indiscernible French.

We mosey to the barn, where a motley crowd of goats shuffles— some brown, some black, long hair, short hair, straight horns, curly horns. Twelve sheep, the color of dirty snow, cling near the far wall. Mon Rosa, the cow, looms like a matriarch in the back.

Apparently, I'm more than a goatherd. I'm a shepherd and a cow herd with forty-two goats, twelve sheep, and Mon Rosa. The sheep baa-aa as the goats knock against their rope partitions. The only farm animals I've been this close to were at county fairs. I rub my forehead and shake my head. I'm so screwed.

Jacques unties the ropes, shooing the tribe up the trail behind the barn. "*Allée!*" he shouts. "*Allée!*"

On this scorching hot September day, the herd and I scale a hillside where sage sprouts in scented patches. Natasha, the herd dog, barks, dancing around us. Most of the goats trot to a cluster of trees, barely taller than I, where they hoist their legs to chomp the leaves and nuts. A tiny caramel goat with stubby legs finds broken limbs on the ground. His legs don't reach high enough up the trunk. The sheep remain glued together, nibbling the grass.

Jacques chews a piece of straw the color of his tussled hair. He points south, where the white zig zags of the Pyrenees Mountains spread over the horizon, dividing France and Spain and little Andorra. The 11,000-foot peaks rise like extended fingers, reaching towards the sky from the earth.

I don't believe in a patriarchal God, but I believe in something, and I am filled with that something's presence. The air and the earth and the goats and the great white Pyrenees' are all One. A soft breath washes over me, giving me an eloquent sense of belonging. The goats' bells ring like a Buddhist's call to meditation. I believe I am supposed to be here, here more than any place in the world. It is this feeling that has no words, but possesses me, that keeps me on the farm, even when the world crashes around me.

Jacques notes the sun's position overhead, his way of telling time. "*Allée!*" Jacques calls to Natasha, the sandy-colored mutt who nips the ankles of the straggling goats. The sheep follow like one wiggly worm trailing behind.

When the goats are installed in the barn, I head to "*Le toilet.*" Outdoors, behind a flowered curtain attached to the house, two boards straddle a stinking, shit-filled, half wine barrel. "*Le toilet.*" I sit on the planks, watching rabbits munch lettuce in their cage opposite my "seat." I rest my elbow on my knee, my chin in my hand, feeling not fear, but wonder and amazement. Life on the farm is like wearing a veil. I never know quite what is going on.

"*Allée*" I call to Natasha, my first time herding by myself. The dog chases the goats to trees that border a stream, where Jacques directed me to go. The consummate student, I extract from my backpack my current novel, *Lost Horizon,* a book of spiritual writings, my French text, my tape for learning French, and my tape recorder. I fold my blue LL Bean jacket over a rock and sit, rubbing the scratchy head of the *petit* goat who cannot reach the tree branches. He wiggles his baby horns, little nubs, into the pages of my book, laying his head on my lap. Each day I read, I study, I meditate. I close my eyes, repeat a mantra, absorb the spirit that emanates from the land. I'm like a monk, more alive than ever before. There is only one problem—the goats. I'm supposed to be a goatherd.

One afternoon I open my eyes from my meditation. "Oh, shit! My goats are gone—again!" Goats often strayed, but usually they stayed in sight. Not today. I might be a devoted spiritual student, but I'm not much of a goatherd. "Natasha," I shout. "Allée! Find them!" Raindrops drizzle from the pewter sky as Natasha flies down the ravine. The goats bellow, emerge from the trees, stampeding towards me to escape Natasha, who gnaws at their hooves. Phew. Everyone's back and accounted for.

A few days later, cold rains plaster me and my charges as we flee another storm. I burst into the kitchen and shake the water off my coat, surprised to see a young man with sharp, blue eyes and a dimpled chin standing next to Camille.

"This is Randy, our new goatherd." First I panic, thinking he is here to replace me. Camille explains they'll use two goatherds, one to herd, one to make cheese, mend, chop wood, and so forth. Sometimes we'll herd together.

My new colleague is small: five feet tall and ninety pounds, the same size as his brothers who are horse jockeys, back in Australia. Randy and I are stark contrasts. I am the carefree,

broad-minded American. I see "the big picture," and sometimes skip the details. With my dark hair and average build, I tower over eighteen-year-old Randy. While I've been in school most of my life, learning from books and teachers, he's grown up on a sheep station outside of Melbourne, tending his father's 2,000 sheep. However, we both speak English. That is enough for a complicated friendship.

During Randy's first week, we herd together. "You're Harrison," he addresses a mahogany goat with white splotches. "See," he turns to me, "his hair is longer than anyone else's. 'Hairy Harrison' we'll call him."

I unpack my books and begin to read. "Hey, have you read this one about the British guy who finds Shangri-la?" The goats' bells jingle as they shake their heads, ruminating.

Randy lowers a pine branch for all the goats who can't the reach leaves. He brushes the bearded tufts of a small-eyed doe. "Look at her chin. We'll call her 'Chinny,'" he says, gathering nuts from the ground which he stuffs in his pockets.

"I mean, it's such a cool book," I say, "about this guy in the sacred mountains in Tibet." The goats nuzzle my fellow goatherd while he hugs them and doles out the nuts. I stop reading, gaze at Randy, then the goats. They dig their noses into his pocket, searching for treats while he cuddles them like they're his children. Okay, I say to myself. So much for my books. It's been fun reading, but…. I stand, wipe the dirt off my pants, and stuff *Lost Horizon* back in my pack. "Let's call this one with the perky little horns 'Baby,'" I say. Baby likes to strut with the larger goats, but he barely keeps up. Already my favorite, he marches with attitude, his head stretched high like a giraffe. He doesn't know he's the runt.

Randy squats next to an older, graying goat with curved horns. "Look at these ankle sores. They're from the dog. You know, we should never use Natasha." In one day, my fellow goatherd knows more about the goats than I've learned in a month. Randy acts reserved with me and the Fontaines, like a cantankerous old gentleman at a London men's club, harping on the woes of the world, sitting in an armchair with a tight collar and cigar. With the goats, though, he's warm, gentle, and more aware than I'll ever be.

Goat herding takes on a new dimension. We name all the goats, becoming like parents to our frisky kids. When the goats play, jumping against each other like Sumo wrestlers, I check to make sure no one gets hurt. I discover who loves nuts and who prefers leaves. I note Chuck, an older goat, has glassy eyes, as though he's going blind. I pocket nuts to urge the goats to come without Natasha. But mostly I spoil Baby, feeding him extra nuts and carrying him when he's too tired to keep up.

One November evening, when screeching winds seep through the windows, Randy and I hunker before the fire. In mid-sentence, Randy interrupts himself and dashes out the back door. I lean against the mantel, baffled, as the fire spins gold curls. A half-hour later, I snatch my coat from the peg and race to the barn. My friend squats in the back, glowing in the lantern's light. "Chuck's barely breathing," the young man says, "I don't think he'll make it through the night." I cough at the stench of the goat's urine in the hay. Chuck's stomach rises and falls like a broken bellows.

"How did you know he was so sick?"

Randy pins his eyes on mine, then focuses on the goat. Randy and the Fontaines have a sixth sense that beguiles me. The spiritual awareness I felt on the mountains my first day is an intuition, instinct, and awareness that grows from living closely with the earth and animals. Randy and the Fontaines tell time without a clock, they know when an animal is sick, they have dreams which foretell the future. They accept and are attuned with nature in a way I never saw in the city.

Chuck dies. His body becomes stew, leather, and goat's head soup. I mourn him, my first death on the farm.

As November rolls into December, winds attack without mercy. Snow and rain assault us. By mid-December, snow climbs halfway up our calves. I bundle myself in scarves and hats and boots, but still, I shiver. I brace myself against a tree for protection from the gales that lash like a master's whip. The snow reaches Baby's belly, so I hold him, my hands blue under torn gloves. Winds rip branches, snap them off their trunks. I yearn for the fire. The days grow darker. We herd for shorter hours. In the worst blizzards, we feed the animals hay in the barn. We trek the mountainside to carry water from a stream since our truck is plugged with ice. Still, I'm learning something I can't put my finger on, something ethereal. I carry two buckets with no problem now. I work more quickly. A kernel within me is blossoming.

A week before Christmas, I wake to sunshine. We haven't seen that golden fire for a month. I dance to the barn, eager to guide my goats. "Baby will stay home this morning," Jacques says. My flock and I barrel up the path, delighted by the warmth and the respite from the wind. At lunchtime, I nestle my goats, sheep, and cow back in their makeshift stalls.

Before dinner, Randy and I haul full buckets from the stream, talking, laughing. "Hey, where's Baby?" I ask.

Randy is silent. Then, "A family bought him today."

"Bought?" My mind acts like a winter tempest, flashing thoughts like lightening; I barely see. I put my pail down. My chest contracts. I scream inside myself, my agony pounding, echoing back. I gasp for air. I can't speak.

Randy hesitates, then lifts his eyes.

"He's going to be someone's Christmas dinner."

I pick up my bucket and start moving. It's easier not to feel while I am walking, but still, tears flood my cheeks. My "Baby" is going to be someone's dinner.

My feet move faster, slipping on the hard, packed snow. I unlatch the kitchen door, and pour the buckets of water into the cauldron while the goats' bells chime like a carillon on Sunday morning.

My Colombian Assignment
By Johna Beall

THE DARK RECESSED GLASS DOORS GO UNNOTICED BY MOST, a cave easily missed in the jungle of Miami airport vendors, employee offices and workrooms. The occasional businessman disappears into the alcove, or a well-dressed group pushing through the narrow opening with a trolley piled high with luggage and shopping bags from Saks or Neiman's.

One of those tall, dark suited businessmen follows me as I enter this steel and glass passageway to the airline lounge, dressed in a charcoal gabardine suit. You can tell the businessmen headed for the Andes by the wool suits. This guy doesn't have a hair out of place or a bead of sweat. Handsome, smooth as silk.

I show my membership card to the woman at the entry desk, all part of my monthly routine flying to Bogotá, Colombia to check the family farm. I ask if the flight is on schedule for 9:30 am. She nods yes, and then I hear from behind me, "Excellent, I hate delays!"

I see him wave his gold lifetime membership card towards her as he glides up beside me, smiling with just the right mix of confidence and gracious courtesy. Very continental.

"May I pour you a cup of coffee? I too am flying to Bogotá this morning. You look so beautiful in that green with your eyes. It would please me to sit with you." I keep walking, reminding myself of my vow not to get involved with Colombian man. I head towards the smell of strong fresh coffee. The compliment is nice; and it's a bit safer to talk to strangers in this lounge. Divorced with three kids, living on an island in Puget Sound, it's not easy to meet men back home. I still respond to flattery. I'm not dead yet, though my ex has given it his best shot.

I smile. Heading to a window seat, he is still with me. "Coffee? I will bring it to you."

"Mmmmm, thank you." He has a lovely deep voice, I think to myself.

He comes back carrying two cups of coffee with cream, sugar and spoons on fine china saucers. "I would love to sit with you. Promise me you will not speak about automobile manufacturing." He says, standing, holding the cups of coffee waiting for my response. "I've had a busy trip to our headquarters in Detroit. I would love a conversation about anything but the car business."

His English is formal, his smile compelling. He seems to understand a bit about North American women. I observe him, smiling despite myself.

"Let me introduce myself properly," He continues, and puts down the coffee. Reaching into his suit jacket he pulls out a business card with flourish. With educated polish he introduces himself, "Luis Cabrera Delgado, CEO of Ford South America. May I sit?"

"Yes." I take his card with a glance, and turn to the window. I am lonely, but worried about making another bad decision with men. I scan the expansive cargo hangers, a few desolate palm trees amidst the chaos of the busy airport loading areas. Waves of heat already coming up from the tarmac. There are massive loads of cargo coming and going into the huge hangers of import businesses crawling with forklifts, pallets loaded, trucks coming and going. The Cargo area in Miami is its own small city. Another familiar jungle: I'm scanning for our fresh roses.

"Yes, it would be good to relax." I say turning to him. "No discussion of possible freezing weather in the next month in Bogotá before Valentine's Day. I don't want to think about our holiday rose crop, worry about aphids or thrips, or cocaine being smuggled with our shipments out of Bogotá. No complaints about the number of flower farms now spread over the Bogotá savannah."

"Of course not." He smiles back to me. "I would never complain about a beautiful woman bringing more flowers, more beauty into this world." He leans closer and looks with me in silence for a moment at the cargo area. Then, "Are you hungry?"

I swallow hard, taking a minute to remind myself, he's talking about breakfast.

The time flies until our boarding call as we get to know each other. He steps away at one point to make arrangements to be seated together on the flight. I am flattered. He is older than me, and he has the powerful magnetism of a very successful man. I relax a bit because he is so courteous. Walking to the airplane with another adult? It's been a while since I've done that.

"How long have you been coming to our beautiful city?" he asks me after takeoff.

"My first trip was in 1980. I came along with my older sister to translate and help with her small children when she moved down. My Dad was here a lot in those days, supervising. I was sick with the lack of oxygen that first time I was here."

He seems interested, so I continue. "My dad was invited to participate in a joint venture starting the rose industry here in Colombia in 1973. Those were the first greenhouses built here, outside the city. He worked with a team of Dutch and Colombian businesspeople. After about a year he went on his own, buying land and planting his own roses. We have the only US owned rose farm in Colombia now."

Luis listens while I describe the family rose farms over 100 years leading to Colombia.

"Right. So you have seen Bogotá grow and improve for the last thirteen years then. Don't you think we are making improvements?" He smiles.

"Yes, there is more development." I continue. "But, on my last trip down I saw a Mercedes limo hit a horse pulling a produce cart. The driver got out, checked his bumper and drove away as the horse lay dying in the street. The level of violence is still shocking. What about the very young girl raped and murdered inside a police station last year?"

He frowns and nods—it was a national outrage.

He puts his hand on my arm and says, "You are picking the worst cases. These problems exist nearly everywhere." His voice is warm, sexy; his touch sends a strong signal through my body.

"Colombia has more murders every year than the rest of the Western Hemisphere put together. It's considered one of the most dangerous cities in the world." I remind him.

"Yes, we have much to do here. We must develop our infrastructure. We must fight crime and corruption, the guerillas, the drug cartel. There are many battles."

Calm and articulate: he tells me about himself. He studied Economics at Georgia Tech, MBA at Wharton. He had been shocked at the racism in the south in the 70's, and the lack of courtesy in North American cities. The irony of this dangerous, violent country: Colombians are more formal than North Americans or many other South Americans.

"The economy here is much better than just five years ago," he continues. "Our people are becoming more educated. The textile industry, your flowers, our manufacturing plant and others like it. We are making life better for the workers. It all takes time."

I look at him thinking, this man has never wanted for anything in his life. He is from one of those few elite families that run the country.

"Come to dinner with me and let me show you the better side of the city." He says as he looks into my eyes, laying his hand on my arm. "Let me show you what is good of this country."

The three-hour flight passes quickly. Our conversation runs from politics to personal details about our families, both of us divorced, with custody issues. I share my background at UC Berkeley and grad school in psychology, how I had ended up running the family business after my father's death. That I care for my mother, preparing the business to sell in five years.

We laugh about how I vaguely resemble the woman on "Who's the Boss?" also syndicated in Colombia. Our workers identify me with that lead character played by Judith Light. It's their shared joke that makes it more palatable to have a blond North American female owner/ manager.

At customs we step through the entry line together. He waits for me to identify my baggage and has his porter pick up my bags to go through the inspection area. Coasting through customs with him is easy, not the usual search through my bags. The officials wave us through smiling. Everyone is glad to see Luis; there's no need for him to go through the formalities.

We step outside into the brilliant sunlight together. I take a deep breath of the thin mountain air. We're at 8661 feet above sea level surrounded by palm trees and bougainvillea. The quaint airport is small by North American standards, needing expansion. The elevated plateau is surrounded by verdant green rolling hills, beautiful foliage everywhere emerging from rich volcanic soils.

Descended from three generations of rose growers, it is in my DNA to love the flowers, the beauty and fertility of this land.

Luis offers me a ride, knowing I'm sure, its hours out of his way. But my driver is waiting: I would have called if there had been a delay in Miami. Luis smiles as my driver steps forward and takes my bags, putting them into the company Toyota Land Cruiser. Ramiro greets me formally and asks if my travels have gone smoothly, in Spanish. Nodding, I ask him how his wife and new baby were doing, and he grins with pride, saying, "*Todo bien, Senora, todo bien, gracias.*"

Luis listens to my Spanish and nods with approval. I'd worked hard to gain that fluency; I always like to see it noticed.

"Dinner on Thursday then? As we agreed? My week will go so much faster!" He says and then bows before turning towards his Mercedes and waiting driver.

I smile and nod, by this time stepping up into the front passenger seat of the jeep for the long bumpy ride to our farm, and the monthly review of farm operations. My week will also go more quickly thinking about our dinner. I smile the rest of the day, thinking of him.

Three days later Ramiro takes me at 8 pm to the small restaurant Luis selected in the fashionable North end.

I'm not sure what is more seductive and intoxicating: the fine wine, his smile, his prestige, the sumptuous French cuisine, his flattery, the candlelit elegant restaurant. I adore everything, *and* the quiet voice in my heart tells me something is wrong. This level of power he has, here, so far from my home: like a wolf afraid to be trapped, I watch nervously.

I know that by the end of the meal I hardly touched, he seems assured that he had made his conquest. He has reserved a room at a nearby boutique hotel, already has the key in his pocket. My seduction is a *fait accompli* in his mind.

At midnight my jeep is not turning into a pumpkin, this prince still at my side, still fawning over me with flattery, a delicate touch and deeply gazing into my eyes. The drive to the hotel does not take long—he had dismissed Ramiro, giving him the address of where to fetch me in the morning. His driver takes us in silence to another elegant location nearby. Luis behaves formally as long as his driver is with us. Alone in the bedroom, the wild animal in him emerges.

Friday morning traffic in Bogotá is as fierce as every other weekday. Ramiro appears at the appointed time, at the hotel to drive me to the farm. Luis will hitch a ride to his factory along the way north from the hotel.

Ramiro's driving seems erratic steering through the usual fierce traffic on Sixth heading away from the hotel. Five lanes of traffic jam into this one way street: we squeeze our way through lines of buses, pedestrians running across traffic, street vendors, horses, taxis, limos, bicycles. This traffic is another element of the urban jungle life I had come to know. A chaos one cannot imagine unless one has driven in a city of seven million in South America.

Ramiro is doing his best to find short cuts, racing down side streets now. I am distracted by Luis's scent and his animal magnetism beside me, basking in his male power.

The squeal of brakes jerks me out of this reverie. There's a terrible thud at the front of the car. "*Dios mio!*" Ramiro utters as he jumps out of the jeep and runs towards the curb.

I also spring into action. When I get to the left front fender looking at the car it seems he has hit something hard, there is a terrible dent, but worse: blood, a wash of blood all over the front left bumper. I scream in English, "Oh God. What have you done?!" Screaming at the sight of the blood first and then of course realizing, I must look down.

"What have you done?" No one answers me; no one hears or acknowledges me.

A circle of people surround the body on the ground, swimming in a pool of blood. But something in me has broken. Why is no one listening? I gaze down at a woman's body. It must be terrible and fatal, a deep injury to the victim's head. No movement. I realize with surprise that the bloodied hair of the victim is blond, so unusual in Bogotá. I see so few blondes, almost never in the course of a day.

A policeman enters the circle around the body and is speaking with Luis. Why don't they hear me? They are leaning close over the body.

Supporting her head carefully, in case there is some life left in her, they turn the body over onto her back. I look down at my own face, awash with blood. Eyes open, staring at Luis, this crowd around me on the street, lifeless. I stare at my own dead body.

A nightmare.

I have awakened covered with sweat, wrapped in the bed sheet, clinching my jaw. I have been crying out to myself in my sleep. I am in the hotel, but there is no man beside me in the bed.

I remember now: sending him away at the door to the room the night before, spending the night alone. He had reserved the room full of expectancy, but politely accepted my refusal to share the bed. I even politely refused his good night kiss. I dress in silence, deeply shaken. Haunted, thinking, *life with Luis would kill something within me.*

I love the idea, but it cannot be.

I descend at 6:30 am to the Land Cruiser down at the curb outside of the Hotel where Ramiro sits in the driver's seat, on time, polite, and respectful as always. He asks me how I am, and I say that I am fine. I ask him how he is and he responds as always, that he is also well.

We ride in silence through the difficult traffic, leaving the city behind. I think of the previous night. I think of my children, the divorce and prolonged custody battle we have recently survived. That I must focus only on my work and parenting. There can be no question of my priority.

I've already made so many mistakes.

Traffic decreases as we exit the city. We pass picturesque farms, small stucco homes with broken tile roofs, cattle grazing, children playing. A starving dog grazes in piles of garbage along the highway. We pass through another small impoverished village and I see our bus loading our workers to get to the farm. The last two miles on a dirt road through the Andes, we caravan slowly to the locked gate where guards wave us through.

Luis calls me later that day while I am in one the greenhouses working with one of the lead growers. I receive the message when I return to the office; thanking the administrator, putting it in my navy blue blazer pocket. The staff watches me with interest, knowing it's impolite to ask about my private life, yet wanting more information. Is he as rich as Ramiro said?

I think about the sensuous setting of jazz and candlelight the night before. I hum to myself one of the songs the sax player played so well: George Benson's "This Masquerade."

The following day there is another call from him, asking to see me before I leave the country. This is a man unaccustomed to rejection. When I did return to the home office, there is another message. He asks me to get back to him, to at least confirm that I arrived safely to my home.

I left a message with his secretary that I had arrived safely.

"No, no other message. Please give him my best. Thank you."

How would I communicate all that I have been through, all that my children have endured? Their stress? The level of hostile scrutiny by my ex and his attorney; the strict requirements to keep shared custody of my children: not what you divulge on a first date. I had only summarized that "the custody battle was prolonged and difficult."

His last message is to call him anytime, whenever I am ready.

But it couldn't work; I would have to give up too much, in so many ways.

My supervisory trips to the farm continued another eighteen months. Rushing through the work to return home to family as fast as possible, I traveled each month quickly and quietly to do my work. I'd happily return to the beautiful Washington woods each time. Striving to better protect my cubs, yet still distracted by that instinct to find the right mate, burning inside.

Moonbeams
By Amber Wong

I CLEARLY REMEMBER THE MOMENT I ACCEPTED my son's inevitable descent into the murk of adolescence. It was a rainy November evening in 2003. Tuesday, the eleventh of November, to be exact. Bryce was 13, he was in middle school, and he had not even started his homework by the time I got home from work. Instead, he sat glued to the TV. Not even looking up from his sprawl on the couch, he confirmed, "Nah, I'm not done," in that maddeningly ambivalent tone that also meant, "and I don't give a $#I%." My shoulders tensed; my head started throbbing. A single parent for eight years, this was going to be one of my rare evenings out. I had plans to attend my niece's baby shower and was looking forward to a nice dinner, an evening of light chatter, and a chance to sit placidly after a long day of heated negotiations at work. I was in no mood to argue tonight.

But this week, I was growing more concerned about Bryce's quarrelsome behavior and his devil-may-care attitude about school. On Monday, the principal had called. Bryce was misbehaving on the school bus—he was getting off at an earlier stop, then running up to his regular stop and then, according to her, dancing in front of the bus. On Tuesday, his science teacher called about one of the pages in his lab book. Apropos of nothing, Bryce had developed a crossword puzzle that included clues to words that were clearly obscene (which, to me, might have been okay, had he not written it into *his lab book*). To top it off, later that evening I'd overheard one of his phone conversations where he was gleefully naming all the girls in his band class who wore thong underwear. When I asked him later, a bit apprehensively, how he knew this, he looked at me like I was an idiot. "Oh, Mom," he sneered in his exasperated *you don't know anything* sort of way, "they do it on purpose. They lean over to pick up their instruments, and, well, you know, it's *obvious*." He was growing more and more headstrong. I had that helpless feeling of losing control.

Now, tonight, it was yet another battle over homework. His insolent response sent me into a tailspin. "Well then," I yelled, in a classic knee-jerk reaction as I grabbed the remote out of his hand and punched the "TV off" button, "you'll just have to go with me to the baby shower!" As my words hung in the air, I immediately regretted them. Why would I bring my teenage son to this quintessentially ladies' event, to a home where I didn't even know the hostess? In that split second, I silently begged him to say, even tersely, "Fine, I'll do it right away if I can just stay home." Instead, he stomped back to his room, emerged with his backpack, and, almost as an afterthought, swept up the newspaper on his way downstairs to the garage. I heard the car door open and slam shut. Then the house was eerily silent.

Stunned, I grabbed the gift and the driving directions and chased after him. Now, we were at a different decision point. At this point, I couldn't back down on my threat and risk him getting out of the car and starting a whole new round of arguments. As I scrambled about, I hurriedly dialed my sister-in-law to make sure it was okay if I brought Bryce. "Of course," she replied brightly, not needing any explanation, "I'll tell Diane." Ah yes, she's a mother of boys. I took a deep breath to calm myself before I hurried down the stairs and slid into the driver's seat next to him. As I backed out of the garage, I sneaked a look. Lips tight, eyes glaring, arms crossed defiantly—this was an all too familiar stance.

We drove in silence for about ten minutes when I realized I had to feed him first. Light tea sandwiches and dessert would not do it for him, or, more importantly, for the hostess. Seizing an opportunity for détente, I stopped at McDonald's for his favorite—the two cheeseburger meal—and remembered to order it just as he liked it, no pickles or onions. He barely looked at me as I handed him the bag. Silently, he wolfed down the entire meal, capped it off with the hollow gurgling noise of a straw. He crammed all the rubbish back into the bag and tossed it on the floor of the car. Then he flipped open the newspaper. I resigned myself to a stony silent drive when I was startled by the sound of his voice. "I need to write about a current event," he said tonelessly. It was so unexpected that it took me a moment to recognize the comment as benign. I sank back into my seat and relaxed my shoulders. We had passed criticality. We had safely moved back into the green zone.

"What's the assignment?" I chirped, a little too thinly. Slowly, carefully, I ratcheted down my hypervigilance of him, concentrating instead on my driving. As I made a right turn, I glanced over at him. That firm set to his jaw had eased. All that chewing and swallowing had relieved his ill humor. Good.

Monotone. "EALRs."

It sounded like "eelers."

Well, that didn't help. Only later would I find out that this stood for "Essential Academic Learnings," which in education-speak refers to broad categories of learning, such as "The student understands and uses different skills and strategies to read." Even when you know what the term means, it doesn't offer any insight on what the student is actually supposed to do to complete the assignment.

"So what do you do for this 'eelers'?"

"Find a current event and write about it."

The headlines that day were about the escalation of the war in Iraq and, more locally, the prosecution of Seattle's most notorious serial killer—the Green River Killer—following a 20-year investigation. Big, meaty, relevant stuff. But Bryce the anarchist had already flipped past those pages. Instead, he was focused on a local news article titled, "Sushi in the Raw: Restaurant's Displays Get Women's Groups Steamed."

Oh *great*. I'd skimmed the article just before heading off to work this morning. A bar in Seattle's Pioneer Square district had been serving up their version of 'naked sushi' since May, and now, six months later, organized protests were materializing.

The article began:

> *"Saturday night at Bonzai in Pioneer Square, a nearly naked woman is laid out on a table. A chef slices sushi behind her, to be arrayed on her torso, bare except for a sheath of plastic wrap and some decorative flower petals. Chopsticks at the ready, patrons line up."*
(Coolican, J. Sushi in the Raw: Restaurant's Displays Get Women's Groups Steamed. *The Seattle Times*. November 11, 2003)

According to the article, the bar owner contended that 'naked sushi', which had been introduced in Japan and was already a mainstay in New York and Los Angeles, was simply performance art. Protesters, mainly Asian-American women, were outraged that it prostituted sushi and exploited women.

"Using chopsticks, they pick among salmon and ahi tuna, eel, and California rolls. The model, one of a rotating group of seven, breathes softly, her eyes closed while she does her 30 minutes of work." (Coolican, J.)

Right from the start, I knew that I couldn't dissuade Bryce from using this article, but as a mom, I had to try. I tried some simple redirection—*what about the article on police forensics, or oh, what about the article on teenage drivers?*—but he stubbornly kept looking down, reading, totally ignoring me. My frustration was mounting, my jaw was tightening, when in a sudden bizarre twist, one of those inexplicable brain farts, the strains of "How do you solve a problem like Maria?" from *The Sound of Music* started streaming, unbidden, through my head. It was so spontaneous, yet so appropriate, that I couldn't help myself—I snorted in laughter. Bryce looked up sharply at the sound but I ignored him and kept my eyes focused dead ahead, desperately trying to stifle a ridiculous grin. In that brief interlude, I raced through the lyrics, hoping that the solution to Maria would magically translate into this situation with Bryce.

How do you solve a problem like Maria?

Many a thing you know you'd like to tell her,
Many a thing she ought to understand.
But how do you make her stay
And listen to all you say?
How do you catch a wave upon the sand?

Oh, how do you solve a problem like Maria?
How do you hold a moonbeam in your hand?

I found perfectly practical questions answered in soaring rhetoric. In short, I got nothing.

"Okay," I relented, lifting my hand from the steering wheel to physically wipe away the traces of the silly smile still lingering on my face. A deep breath. "Okay, then let's talk about this article. Why do you want to write about this article?"

He glanced over at me to see if I was kidding. I was not. I had put on my best "interested parent" face. He looked back down and, testing his victory, continued reading. "Because it's funny, that's why," he declared.

"Yeah, you're right." In my mind, détente warranted a little affirmation. Then, forcing a light tone and trying to sound neutral, I continued, "So do you think that the women doing the naked sushi think it's funny?"

"Huh." A pause. *Good. Maybe he's thinking about it.* He continued scanning the article. "Huh. It doesn't say."

"What do *you* think?"

Pause. "No, I guess."

"Then why do you think they do it?"

"The money, I guess. They probably get paid a lot."

I knew better, but I didn't want to get into a sidebar argument about the economics of women's work vs. men's work, so I stuck to the main topic. "Do you think it's a good way to make money?"

"Sure, it's easy. All they have to do is lie there."

Right, just like prostitutes, I wanted to say. But I restrained myself, bit my lip, tried to find another angle. "Would *you* do it for money?" Softer, conspiratorially, I remind him, "Because it's easy money, like you say."

"*Wha?*" Indignant, "No, of *course* not." He practically spit it out. It's obvious what he was thinking: Guys don't do this. Girls do this. Why does he already think this way? How has he, at 13, already picked up these gender biases?

"So who would want to go to a place like that?"

Now a grin. "A lot of people," he said. "A lot of *guys*," he corrected himself.

"Would you go to a place like that?"

"Sure, why not?" The smug tone was edging in.

"Would you want your girlfriend to do that?"

Out of the corner of my eye, I saw his head jerk up.

This fall, he'd gone through three girlfriends in as many weeks. Although the break-ups, if they can even be called that, seemed like mere blips in the course of his week, at least he had the momentary experience of connection, of empathy. At least, I was counting on that.

"Ahhh, no."

"Why not?" I didn't want it to, but it came out sounding like a challenge.

He felt it. Suddenly, there was a new edge to his voice. "I just wouldn't, *that's all.*" The downward slant to his tone marked a definite end to this discussion.

I waited. I let it sink in. *Now* did he get it? Did he understand how exploitative "naked sushi" was? Did he see these women as connected, as another guy's girlfriend, another guy's sister? Did he just *sense* that it was wrong? Whatever he was thinking, I knew better than to ask. That teachable moment had passed. We'd circled back to a flash point that, if ignited, would utterly ruin the entire evening. I wouldn't be bringing my quiet, unimposing son to this event. I'd be bringing a surly, argumentative teenager. I decided to leave it at that.

After ten minutes of all-too-familiar silence, we reached our destination. In one smooth motion, Bryce shoved the newspaper into his backpack, opened the car door, and as he got out, I thought I heard him mutter, "Thanks, Mom, I know what I want to write now." I swung around in disbelief. *Did he really say that? Was he truly thankful for my attention? Had he actually taken my words to heart?* It took me only a moment to decide to put those questions to rest. Whatever words were carried on the wind, I chose to believe. Because for one brief, shining moment, I felt that elusive moonbeam alight softly in my hand.

Adaptations

By Kellini Walter

MY SISTER RENEE DIED SLOWLY AND THEN ALL AT ONCE.

It started in the spring of 1996 when she saw some unexpected blood in the toilet. She ignored it because she wanted to go to China to adopt a baby girl and she wouldn't face the possibility that she was sick. So later that same year, in June, she flew to China anyway. She brought Lilian home, and six months later, around Lilian's first birthday, she found out she had colon cancer.

Twelve hundred miles, eight years, and a complicated relationship separated us. She was older—as kids that meant she didn't have much to do with me unless she was bossing me around, and as adults we had slipped into a strange, lopsided pattern where I would listen during our hour-long phone conversations but not have much to say in return. A couple of weeks after Renee's initial diagnosis, I was working in my home office when she called.

"We need to talk about something," she said abruptly. "I want Lilian to come live with you."

I got up from the desk and lay down on the floor. I stared up at the beam that ran across the ceiling and tried to sink away. "But Renee, you just found out, and the doctor said there's a lot they can do."

"Look. I'm not going to survive this cancer. I know I'm going to die." I put the phone down next to my ear and closed my eyes while I listened to her words from a distance. "She's still a baby and she will bond with you now. It will be so much harder for her the more attached she gets to me."

I picked up the phone. "Renee. I'm sorry, but this doesn't make any sense to me. The doctor said you have a really good chance. He said early-stage colon cancer has a very high survival rate—especially because you are only forty."

"I have to tell you something else about Dave. I never wanted you to know, but you have to know."

I sat up and leaned back again the wall. Renee's husband, Dave, was weird, but he seemed harmless.

"He's been using drugs—crystal meth. He can't take care of Lilian by himself. You can't tell mom. You have to promise me." Her voice had that tight, controlled tone that always made me anxious.

My carefully worded response did not show my inner thoughts—it was more important to calm her down than blurt out what I wanted to say—"Holy hell, Renee. You knew you could be sick, you knew Dave had a drug problem, and you adopted Lilian anyway?" Instead, I sat up straight and said, "Renee, if you're right and you don't make it, I promise I'll take Lilian. But if I take her now, you'll want her back when you get better."

"I hope to hell you are right. But Dave will never let Mom have her, so you have to take care of her if I die."

We hung up. I shut the door on my office and walked into the great room of my hundred-year-old Victorian apartment. I loved that room. The fireplace, built-in china cabinets, and the wide-plank pine floors made it feel like a country cottage in the middle of my Seattle neighborhood. It was easy to feel real and authentic in this very solitary and uncomplicated life. And when I needed the energy of the city, it was just a few blocks away.

I built a fire and thought about Lilian. With my heavy travel schedule, erratic routine, and general thirty-two-year-old self-absorption, my life wasn't set up for kids. I hadn't ruled out being a mother someday, but I wasn't ready to become one anytime soon.

There was a chance Renee was right—maybe she could sense her fate. But the timing felt so wrong to me. If I were meant to raise Lilian, I would—but I wasn't ready to deal with the reality of that—yet.

After that phone call and before I even understood what happened, I subconsciously faced the truth and let go of my grip on an easy, single life and made choices that created a more grown-up existence. By the time I was thirty-five, I'd taken a stable job at Microsoft, fallen in love with an amazing man—Jake—and we'd bought and begun to fix up a cute little bungalow.

The day I left to fly to Nebraska to be with Renee in her final hours, Jake and I went for a walk. I had delayed this conversation until the last possible moment because I was terrified he might decide to leave. About three blocks down, I slowed a little. "Jake. You need to make a decision about what you want to do."

"What do you mean?" His dark eyes were sweet but anxious as he squinted against the summer sun.

I stopped walking because the task of talking suddenly seemed too daunting to coordinate with my body in motion. Words spilled out in the rushed torrent of a semi-rehearsed speech. "Look," I said as I averted my gaze and stared down at the ground. "In a few hours, I'm going to get on a plane and go be with my sister until she dies. Then I'm going to pack up Lilian and bring her back to raise her." I paused for a moment and drew in a very deep breath and breathed in the scent of freshly mowed grass. "I made this choice before we met. You have to make your own choice."

He grabbed my hand and said, "I'm doing this. If you're doing this, I am doing this. We are doing it together."

Three-and-a-half-year-old Lilian came home with me five days later, and we muddled through the early weeks of our life together. We watched *The Sound of Music* over and over again. It was the only kid movie we owned. Our family soon grew after Jake and I loosely and theoretically discussed that it would be good to have other children soon, so the age difference wouldn't be too big between Lilian and her younger siblings. That led to just one moment of "No, don't stop," and Olive was born in October 2000 on the third anniversary of the day Jake and I met—just sixteen months after Lilian had arrived.

We decided that I would continue to work at Microsoft and Jake would continue to work as a stage actor and be a stay-at-home dad. We both loved the unconventionality of that choice, and we underscored it with the idea that we didn't really need to get married. We were in love and our relationship had already survived so much. What did it matter if we got married? We felt more married than many married couples we knew.

I pushed myself through the days of the years. There was an overwhelming amount of work to do—a crazy, full-time job, groceries, laundry, healthy meals, complicated schedules, and the real-time emotional needs of Jake and the girls were the stones across the river of my life that I leapt frantically across. To survive, I anchored everything around my complete faith that the bond between Jake and me would buoy our family and keep us going. I clung to that belief for a very long time—until a different, contradictory truth began to appear around the edges of our life.

In the summer of 2008, we were in Central Oregon for Jake's annual family reunion. We always looked forward to this weekend. I loved spending time with Jake's Aunt Tina, and he loved two mellow days where he could sit for hours and catch up with a small group—ten or so—of his favorite relatives.

The first night at around 10:00, I looked over at seven-year-old, bleary-eyed Olive and decided to get the girls back to the hotel.

I found Jake in a plastic chair under the lawn tent with his cousins Brett, Melanie, and Greg. As I asked if he was ready to go, Jake's eyes looked up at me with disappointment. I knew he could happily hang out for a few more hours. "The girls are beat. If you want to stay I can take them back to the hotel. You can get a ride with someone else."

He set his plastic glass of wine in the grass and started to get up. "No. Let's go."

The gravel in the driveway crunched under our feet as we made our way past an RV and around the few cars that remained from the first night of the weekend-long party.

Jake stumbled as we felt our way past a pick-up truck, and I realized he had been drinking for almost six straight hours. I thought about this and asked him, "Are you ok to drive?"

"I'm fine," he said defiantly.

The girls pulled their weary bodies into the back seat of the car as I buckled into the front seat. The smell of rancid white wine joined Jake in the driver's seat. I heard my therapist's voice in my head "*But you don't let him drive with you or the children in the car when he's been drinking?*"

"*We'll be fine. It's a short drive to the hotel,*" was the thought of denial that glazed over the surface of my fear.

"Did you have a good time?" he asked expectantly as we started slowly down the rural driveway.

"I was bored," said seven-year-old Olive said from the back seat.

He started in, "It's your family. You should enjoy hanging out with them." I thought of ways to shut this down as quickly as possible.

"She's tired. We've had a long day. It's ok." Tactic number one—inspire empathy. Tactic number two—distraction: "Do you know when Penny and Dereck are coming tomorrow? Are they caravanning with Val and Andrew?"

"I don't know what those guys are doing. You know Andrew; he'll decide tomorrow morning."

We bounced through the ruts in the country road. "Can you please take it easy? We aren't in any hurry."

He was annoyed. "It's fine. Relax."

I closed my eyes and took a deep breath as we turned onto the paved road that would take us to the highway. The buttes on the right and the sprinkling of farmhouses on the left moved past quickly. We curved around the final stretch that led to the T intersection with Highway 26. Instead of slowing down, he seemed to be speeding up.

I looked around; maybe I was disoriented, maybe we weren't as close to the highway as I thought, but it looked right, it looked like... the stop sign was right in front of us now... "JAKE!" He brought the car to a stop midway through the quiet intersection. "Jesus Christ, what were you doing?"

"I'm sorry, it just came up on me sooner than I expected."

"What's wrong?" Lilian said sleepily from the back seat.

"*Your dad almost killed us,*" is what I wanted to say, but that would have required the adrenaline blasting through my veins to purge my deep trenches of restraint. "It's ok. We'll be at the hotel soon."

As Jake slowly navigated us back into the right lane, the hotel was in sight. And as if by osmosis, I soaked up the desperate thoughts of an alcoholic and said to myself, "*Never again. Tomorrow I quit. I won't let him drive drunk with the girls and me ever again.*"

The next night, around the same time, the party had dwindled down to the four cousins who would spend the night in tents or RVs and us. Jake was in the same spot, and we had the same conversation as the night before. But this night, on the walk to the car, I said, "I have the keys. I'll drive."

"I'm fine," he said insolently.

"You have been drinking in the hot sun all day. I haven't and I'm driving."

"Kellini, give me the keys."

"No."

He was still silently angry the next morning. I needed to leave by 11:30 so I had time to travel to the airport to catch a flight for a business trip. At 11:45, we pulled out of the hotel parking lot. A couple of blocks later, he suddenly jerked the car over and parked.

"What are you...?"

"I'm getting ice cream."

"Ice cream?!" the girls squealed in unison from the back seat. They were as surprised as I was. He never liked to stop in the beginning of a trip, and he often lectured all three of us about the evils of sugar.

"But we are running late and I..." He was already out the door as I started to protest. I sat in silence and wondered if this was what it seemed, that he was deliberately going out of his way to show me he was in control.

Over the next two years, we gradually moved into separate corners. I withdrew from his anger and disappointment, and he walked toward a daily dance with alcohol. The final moment came when we were with a couple's counselor, and she asked me if I felt like Jake had my back. I thought about how it seemed like I often set him off with random things I said or did. I thought about the times he told me he was thinking of leaving. And I thought about how I felt I'd done everything I could to keep the family going, only to sense that it wasn't enough, that *I* wasn't enough. And I spoke my unforgivable truth, "No."

Six months after we split up, I found myself climbing up a ladder. I held tightly to a garden hose with my free hand. Since I didn't feel solid enough to climb one foot over the other, I stepped both feet onto a rung before moving higher. When the moss-covered roof came into view, the challenge of doing something that Jake used to do held the promise of a small advance in the war against my heartbreak. My breath swirled around my face and fogged up my thick glasses on the cold December morning. I stopped to steady myself, reached out, and began to spray. The damp smell of Seattle filled my nostrils as the water worked its way to the place where the stubborn clumps of thick moss clung to the roof. I remembered what Jake had said to me before he left: "You will survive this. That's what you do: you survive."

As I worked off the moss, I replayed the drama with Lilian from the night before. "You can go to the party and spend the night at Emily's, but I'm going to pick you both up when the party is over at 12:00." I had a funny feeling about her fifteen-year-old plans for the evening. I would let her do what she said she was going to do, but I would create a potential speed bump if I wasn't getting the whole story.

"Why?" Her black eyes pierced through me as though I had asked her to cut off a finger.

"I just want to check in with you at the end of the evening before you go to Emily's. Why is that a problem?"

"Because we already have plans for a ride home."

"I don't think Emily's parents will mind not picking you up. They picked you up from the last party."

"Emily's parents aren't picking us up."

"But you said…"

"No, I said we had a ride."

"So who is the ride?"

"Sam."

"Well, I'm sure Sam's parents won't mind if they don't have to bring you home."

"I DON'T WANT YOU TO PICK ME UP."

"Why?"

"Because I DON'T WANT YOU TO PICK ME UP."

She started to cry a little the way she does when she is caught in a lie. Finally, she said something I believed. "Because the party doesn't get over until 1:00."

It was a small lie—that the party ended at 1:00 instead of 12:00. But even a little lie wasn't ok. She didn't go to the party.

After she stormed up to her room, I sent Jake a text message to tell him what happened. For three weeks, we'd barely communicated with each other, and I wondered how he would respond. I hit Send on the text message and felt the emotional gut punch that rendered me breathless. I hated going through these moments alone.

His response surprised me. "I totally agree with you. I know this was really difficult but you did the right thing." It was normal for him to say something like this when it came to the girls. But over the course of the difficult, often irrational, and irrevocable conversations that lined the path to our break-up, I had lost touch with how well he was able to steady me when I had doubts as a mother. And in the midst of the chaotic emotions that arrive when love seems to have either departed or never existed at all, I had almost forgotten how kind he could be.

I watched the moss slush toward the edge of the roof and I thought about how much I missed Jake and our promise of forever. Then I reminded myself that the only forever we had left was as parents. He was right. I would survive. I had always been able to stand on the ledge of my life and hang on. But I wondered—could there be something more?

Grace

By Carmen König D'Arcangelo

From the driver's seat I slam the door of the Volvowagon shut. It brings me right back to another door, another life…

***

The large wind-worn oak gate clinks shut as I enter the house of my weekday caregivers. Herr und Frau Jahn live in a tiny hamlet outside of Stuttgart, Germany. My maternal grandmother delivers me on Sunday night and I live with the Jahns until pick-up on Friday after school. Often my grandmother and I steal through the thick evergreen woods connecting Station #73 to the two bedroom shack the Jahns rent.

I know Gypsies squat in these woods, eating charred cat meat over their silent fires. I hear stories of furious dancing amidst loud chanting, a kaleidoscope of skirt colors whirling through the silent fires.

"Don't worry *kleine* Carmen, we are walking briskly, people think we have a place to go," my grandmother assures me.

We walk alone in the heavy starless night, a sixty year old golden-trussed woman and the six year old granddaughter she has been assigned to rear. Stumbling, I follow the yank of her calloused hand.

***

The Jahns' house is self-contained amidst the ambling farmland. Wild columbines, rosehips (for making tea) and morning glory tumble out from every corner of the large overgrown yard. A hidden space. The backyard opens into a 12x10 chicken coup and two dilapidated bunny hatches. Two three inch iron poles stand tall beside the back porch door and serve to anchor the laundry line. I will spend hours slowly climbing up and down, latching my thin panties around the pole in naïve rapture. The effervescence of internal fires blushing my cheeks. Too early. Too urgent.

Next to the chicken coup lives a one-room garden shed that the landlord frequents during the hot southern German summers. He invites me in offering chocolate and greedy hands. His woolen suit is rough against my knees. His thighs are old, feeble and tired. I feel a tinge of electricity as the sweetness of cocoa floods my mouth. And I remember the pungent smells his fingers generate. They tumble into the room and mixing with the earthly smells of a working farm; warm chicken bodies, sweet goat milk and yesterday's cigarettes. The sounds of a man, surely in his 80's, lost amidst the random clucking of chickens. No one is watching. No fingers of protection reach through the unlocked door. I live in a world immune from my control.

***

My maternal grandmother, Oma, raises me for the first eight and a half years of my life. *It takes a village.* My village is composed of Oma, my mother's gregarious and charming younger sister, Gerlinde, and the weekday foster care arrangement with Herr und Frau Jahn. My biological parents reside in a small town in Vermont.

"You are marrying an *Ami*. Why can't you choose an upstanding German man?" barks my grandmother.

My parents meet at Kelly Barracks, a U.S. military installation in Stuttgart, where they are both employed. He is an enlisted soldier with a specialty in journalism and she an indigenous, civilian secretary. In rebellious love they marry against the will of my grandmother. Nine months to the day I arrive.

The desperately-clung-to family line is that my grandmother is better equipped to raise me in those early years. After all she has two jobs, an apartment and experience with child rearing. My parents are twenty-three years old, unemployed and looking for an apartment. My father is fleeing assignment to Vietnam and returns to the United States shortly after I am born. There is a black and white scrap of a photograph where he is holding an infant-me. For many years this is all I know of him.

My mother stays on only to walk across a red light in a busy intersection. She is thrashed by an eight-wheeler truck puncturing one lung and diagonalizing her right knee. Six months of hospitalization and recovery follow. I remember a picture of my mother propped up with white linen pillows on my grandmother's couch wrapped in a hip to toe cast. I lie next to her on the featherbed as she looks into the camera with a faint, tired smile. Upon recovery my mother follows her husband to the United States-toward freedom. I am left—a token of the past. Soon they will call for me.

***

Living with Oma has its upsides. First, she inhabits a furnished apartment on the twelfth story of an old beige brick building with a view to the subway. There is a tiny glassed in veranda where my beloved blue parakeet Willie lives-and dies. I remember weeping over the toilet as my grandmother flushes him away. Attachment comes and goes immune from my control. That night I wet my bed.

For many, uncountable mornings I awaken to a drenched, clinging nightshirt. My grandmother, with whom I share a bed, darts out of our king-size mattress with a grunt of disapproval.

"*Nicht wieder*," not again, she sputters.

A penetrating acrid smell hangs in the air as I am flung out from the sheets. The wetness clings to the bed frame creating a flopping, slapping sound as the sheets are crumpled into a ball. The rustling sound of tepid bath water running drowns out my grandmothers annoyed sighs. This scene is familiar, often repeated. I sit, still moist from the bath but fully dressed, as my grandmother presents our daily breakfast; a soft boiled egg with untoasted buttered rye bread. Oma cooks a marvel of an egg. Perfect really: thermally hot and just the right drip of softly warm yolk. Every morning, constancy in a shell. But amidst the predictability lives an internal fear, palpable yet undefined.

In intervals my mother and father send brown paper wrapped packages and money from the U.S. I recall receiving an off-white plastic telephone that clicked delightfully when you turned the dial. I talk incessantly on that phone. "Hallo, anyone out there? Anyone." I squeeze my eyelids shut imagining America and trying to draw a visual of my parents.

At four, dialing that play telephone, I question nothing. I was an orderly, well-mannered little German girl. My grandmother with her perfectly manicured dentures would have it no other way. At sixty, she will not to be upstaged by parenting a toddler. She works hard all her life yet her steely fingers sparkle with sophistication- a different glimmering jewel on each finger.

In the early 70's in Germany, it takes two salaries to raise a family. As our family's breadwinner, Oma cleans during the day and bartends at night and on weekends to make ends meet. Fridays we ride the subway to our apartment and then later to the train station where she bartends. The wet glasses clatter as they are dunked, lifted and stacked with the endless repetition of a Guttenberg press. I'm perched snuggly on a stool in a remote corner of the train station eatery. The neon sign flashes *Kammers.*

***

I attend first and second grade in Germany. I learn about the birds and the bees. I study religion, handwriting and math. I spend an overnight at my second grade teacher's house, why I don't recall. She serves up spinach and cheesy eggs and a conventional husband and wife family structure.

Weekend days are my favorite time of the week. Oma is off from work until the evening and the days languish with ordinary household tasks and visits from my Aunt Gerlinde. Her ebullient and often dramatic presence intrigues me. On good days, she laughs lightly and walks with youthful elegance through our apartment. Other days, she cries and chain smokes effusively. I look up to her, a divine fusion between sister and mother.

One of these lazy afternoons is interrupted by a telephone call from the U.S. Usually I am too absorbed in talking on my own telephone (*Hallo-anyone out there?)* to notice these weekly calls from my mother. This call stops me.

"I don't understand, Renate. She is so happy and settled here." My grandmother's tone is urgent.

I cock my head and listen intently, pretending to speak to an imaginary caller.

"I will take care of her without any payment. Germany is her home. She is living here now and we are taking good care of her," Oma sputters.

There is a long listening silence. My eyes dart over to my grandmother. Her face awash in a stream of tears and her fingers tap out piano chords on the table; a habit she has when nervous. Suddenly, she slams the telephone down and leaves the room.

In the days that follow my German village mobilizes into action. Oma and Linde make copious calls to the U.S to persuade my mother to keep me with them. They offer to pay for all my expenses. The Jahns' offer to take care of me for free. Letters are written. I felt quite important and quite expensive. By now I am eight years old and have impeccable penmanship thanks to my rigorous German schooling. I decide to write my own letter.

Dear Mom and Dad,
I really appreciate all you have done for me. the packages, the gifts, the money. I really do. But I love Oma and she is taking really good care of me. Herr und Frau Jahn are willing to take care of me for free. I really like horseback riding near their house. This next year in school I will be able to take swimming and English so I can talk with you and Dad even better. Tante Gerlinde is willing to help Oma take care of me. Germany is my home. I will be very, very good. I promise. I want to stay. Please don't take me away.
Your daughter,
Carmen

I carefully fold the letter, unfold it and read it again. Had I been respectful? Had I said all the things that were important? I decide to plant a row of red hearts on the bottom of the page for emphasis. I lick the envelop shut and carry it to the mailbox at the bottom of our building twelve stories down. It grows heavier in my hand with each step I take. I wipe a wet drop from the envelope before sliding it into the mail slot.

Two weeks later my grandmother accompanies me on a Lufthansa flight to Boston. I haul a small suitcase with clothes and my favorite doll Anita. Most of my belongings, including my off-white plastic telephone, remain in Germany. My grandmother and I stand frozen; incredulous at the choices being made outside our control. I am drunk with indecision.

***

"Your Grandmother is always with you. She is your Guardian Angel," the voice jolts me back to the present.

I am perched in the driver's side of the Volvo telephoning with my *fortune teller*, Maria. Visions of dark backrooms, angular features and hoarse voices come to mind. Maria is not that fortune teller. She is practical, direct and funny; a no nonsense muse.

Misty sprays drift in through the open driver's side window. It is 8:33 am on an autumn Sunday in Seattle. This morning we discuss recent travails; two moves, the death of two cats in two weeks, a stolen car, a struggling marriage. And as always we settle in with my Grandmother.

"Your grandmother is always with you. She wants you not to worry and is there to reassure you that everything is going to be alright," she continues.

I drift away to a moment two years earlier. I am describing my grandmother to the Lutheran priest who will eulogize her.

***

"Ahhhh.......That is very interesting," says the priest directing his piercing eyes towards me.

Twenty-two hours of car and plane travel finds me, a forty-two year old mother of three, sitting in the small bosom of my maternal family of origin. We are seated around the table feeding slices of our experience with my grandmother to the priest. Four days ago she died with angel kisses on her cheek, my aunt and me by her side.

"When a child is raised by a grandparent they often know the grandparent more authentically than anyone else. How would you describe your grandmother, Carmen?" he asks.

Before I can speak, my mother jumps in.

"My mother and I rode the trains from East German to the West. We collected snails together in the West and we were happy to have them. When I married Gary and moved to the United States, I left her my best belonging-my daughter," she finishes sitting back, hands folded, on the crushed velour couch.

I look down, shoulders heavy with the relentless burden of this frequently recited story. I feel queasy, seduced by the spinning little dragons in my stomach that want to lurch out and scream-*That is the most ridiculous excuse for not being a parent I have ever heard.* I hide them away. I wonder if anyone else hears the dragons. The priest keeps his attention on me.

"How did you experience your grandmother as a human being?" he follows up.

The reality is I *do* know my grandmother. A shard of rose quartz polished by the weather of time and hardship. Artistic, enduring, passionate, hard working, opinionated, deeply loyal; I thread a necklace of virtues and personality traits for the priest. She was a survivor of two world wars without hiding from herself or anyone else. She did not keep silent. She rallied against my mother marrying an American. She despised having to send me, her oldest granddaughter, to the United States. She stood firmly in the reality of her own life and through her actions forced other to stand in theirs.

Hers was a life of owning the risks we take in a world mostly immune from our control. A life of grace.

***

"You can always connect with your grandmother –she is in the physical and she is always near," Maria tells me.

I look up and a slight hint of rainbow crosses the concrete sky. I remember to ask Maria about the complicated weave of love and attachment and protection. We cover vast swaths of territory: maternal love, spine tingling first loves and memories of "puppies in love" affairs from eighteen years ago. She does not know the future of my marriage. I think about grace and love. There is no control in love.

"People are placekeepers in our lives –until the right person comes along. I'm not saying your husband is not the right person but the timing is not right now," she continues.

A familiar aching wave of helplessness snaps itself onto my body.

"Remember Carmen-she is your Guardian Angel and she will hold your place in the world," Maria concludes.

I drive off grounded in the soft mountain of maternal reassurance; open, vulnerable to oxygenated life. I drive off in an unusual state of confidence and inner peace. The kind of sleepy peace you have after hours of lovemaking. The road winds home through a neighborhood I'm slightly familiar with. I suddenly decide to turn into a coffee shop. Had I noticed it before? I step inside and walk toward the gleaming glass pastry counter.

"What is good here?" I ask.

"I recommend the fruit tart," a voice calls.

"Oh yes?" I turn to look at the voice.

People are placekeepers.

No Man's Land

By Lauren McGuire

HOME DOESN'T EXIST, NOT SINCE MY BROTHER killed a drag queen with a samurai sword. Worthington, Ohio is still on the map. It's not destroyed like New Orleans or Tikrit, Iraq. I lived in Worthington while I was in middle and high school, and I haven't lived there since I was eighteen when I went to college near Chicago. I never was one of those people who hated Ohio, I just found something better, like one who leaves a cute, funny boyfriend for one who is sexy and smart. The first one isn't necessarily bad, but the second is better.

I used to be a favorite daughter of Worthington, a sweet, cozy enclave of the upper-middle class north of Columbus. I liked high school and who I was: student body president, drill team cadette and foreign exchange student. I was studious and friendly, not a snob or part of the clique whose favorite sport was cutthroat socializing.

Worthington theoretically should feel like home, a place I can walk anywhere and feel safe and secure and loved. My friend Elizabeth lives there, around the corner from her mom and dad. My parents still live there. My bedroom is more or less the same as when I left: the poster from the movie *Sid and Nancy* is down, but the single bed with a brass headboard has the same bedspread it did in 1987.

C.P. sent me an email about our twenty-year high school reunion. I hadn't heard about it, as I had moved from Chicago to Saint Louis to Seattle since the ten-year event. We each agreed that we would go if the other one did. My parents would be happy to watch my kids while I was out.

"You look gorgeous!" Theresa gushed as I walked into the reunion, held at the Worthington Hills Country Club. I was wearing a little black dress, silver shoes, and arrived in my father's burgundy Miata. In high school, I had eaten lunch with Theresa every day for three years. When I saw her, I froze and couldn't think of anything we had in common. I let her carry the conversation.

"Do you live in town?" she asked.

"No, I live in Seattle," I replied. "And you?

"Cincinnati," she said.

I relaxed and knew she was safe to talk to. She wasn't in Columbus when my brother made the news, first in 2002 when Michael killed Gary, and then again in 2005 for the trial. All four local televisions stations covered Michael's story, and the Columbus *Dispatch* had a dedicated reporter who showed up every time Michael appeared in court.

Before the reunion, Elizabeth told me "No one will remember what happened. He was arrested five years ago." I thought she was being generous. The day after Michael was arrested, Elizabeth saw Michael on the morning news. Worried, she immediately called my parents.

"The trial was only two years ago," I argued.

"Most people don't follow those types of stories," she said.

"They made a big deal about Michael being from Worthington. People surely caught that."

"Not many people linked you and Michael. You were only in the same school for one year."

Maybe she was right. Nevertheless, I stood close to her and C.P. during the reunion, and mostly talking to people who lived in Pittsburgh or Portland, Toledo or New York. I never inquired about anyone's parents or siblings, for fear they would ask about mine. I avoided most people who went to my parents' church; I was sure the gossip passed from parent to child, likely not including details of my brother's ten-year descent into schizophrenia, or how he thought he was Michael the Archangel and had never been violent before.

Elizabeth cut in on my conversation with Theresa when Kathy walked up to me. She looked exactly the same as she did in high school, including the sandy brown bobbed hair, cream-colored blouse and patterned skirt. She must not have heard about Michael, as she approached me without hesitation.

"Are you a doctor?" she asked.

"No, I studied math in college, but my husband is a doctor," I said. She lives in town, but she must have missed the news since she had been working thirteen-hour days. I pointed her in John's direction, and he was happy to discuss clotted blood vessels and whatnot.

Feeling brave, I walked up to a woman I vaguely knew in high school. "Hi Erin," I said.

She looked terrified. "Are you in Columbus?" she asked.

"Seattle."

"You must talk to Amy. She is in Seattle, too. I saw her over there." She pointed to a table in the distance. By the time I looked in the direction of her hand, Erin was gone.

Amy lives in Portland, but as Cleveland and Cincinnati are inter-changeable to West Coasters, Seattle and Portland are two similarly soggy Pacific Northwest towns to those east of the Mississippi.

"I hated high school. It was a blur. I was glad to leave," Amy said.

"I left Ohio after high school," I said. At eighteen, I needed to prove Worthington wasn't some awful fluke, the only place where I would be liked and be successful. I needed to leave it behind, and I did. I also wanted to return to the Chicago area. Evanston was a home I never knew, where my dad, grandfather, and great-great-grandfathers were born and raised since the 1860's. When I left for college, all of my grandparents lived in Chicago. They were proud of my return.

My husband doesn't understand why I need to come back to Ohio. He grew up in Sioux City, Iowa. We met in Chicago and lived there throughout our twenties. He left Iowa for the big city and never went back, but I wanted to return to the days when I was Student Council President, destined to go to a good college, and have a happy, success-ful life sitting around the corner.

More than a place, home is a time. I long for the time before trag-edy. I long for the days when the most popular boy in the sophomore class had a secret crush on me, and the only reason I knew was because his mother told mine. I don't know if Chris's crush was fact or fiction, or if it was the combined wishful thinking of the mothers of two tal-ented children. At the time I brushed the crush aside. I had an older boyfriend, a senior with a job, a car and a fledging rock band. That, and Chris never talked to me outside of discussions in English class.

I don't yearn for the boy who adored my teenage self, but I want to go back to when I was emotionally available instead of terrified of what people would think of me if they knew Michael's story. I had been full of confidence. I had no secrets and no one looked at me sideways.

I saw Chris at the reunion, and wondered if he knew about Michael given the rapidity at which gossip travels through Worthington. I didn't say hi. I thought if someone were to offer his or her condolences, it might have been him. I didn't want to see the look of relief in his eyes, seeing the girl he hypothetically had a crush on, grateful he avoided her and her crazy family. With less than an hour to go, I left the reunion, relieved I had escaped without talking about my brother.

Three days later, John and I went to Toledo to visit Michael. If Michael were sane and had never killed his friend, perhaps we would have gotten together with his wife and kids at their house. Instead, we saw him in his new home, prison. The rain pounded the car as we drove north. Seventy miles out of town, we stopped at a gas station. The headline from the local newspaper said Findlay had flooded and been evacuated. Near the Blanchard River, tops of tombstones peeked out from a flooded field. Exits were closed along Interstate 75. Mud and rocks and sandy debris were caked on the highway, telling us the road had been covered in water hours earlier. The skies cleared as we approach the outskirts of Toledo.

John and I arrived at the Toledo Correctional Institution. We showed our IDs, went through a metal detector and marched through seven sets of locked doors before we saw Michael waiting for us at a table in the visiting room. Because John and I came from more than 150 miles away, we were allowed to visit the whole day instead of for only a few hours in the morning. A blond, goateed, bespectacled inmate took a picture of the three of us with a digital camera. He wore a wedding ring, and I smiled and thanked him for the picture. He returned the smile with more wattage than I gave: he looked at me as if I was the first person to smile at him in years, as if I could see him for the person he was before his incarceration.

A teenage boy sat in his prison garb, and his parents came to visit. He smiled like a regular kid, and if I weren't in the big house, I would think his parents were buying their college age son lunch while visiting the campus. As soon as his parents left, the boy's eyes turned steely, crossing slightly inward, perhaps skewed by his glasses. The grin was gone, with no trace that it was ever there. Another boy was visiting with his mom and perhaps his grandma and aunt, all with matching bouffants. They were joyous when the pictures of him were taken, as if this were his high school graduation all over again.

Michael complained about his lawyers, insisting that they were incompetent because they tried to get him declared Not Guilty By Reason of Insanity.

"I am fine. They didn't know what they were talking about," Michael said, then paused. "I am not going to talk about it anymore."

I wondered if he would continue the self-defense rant he had been maintaining for the past several years, the paranoid nightmare that Gary killed two of his friends and then wanted to kill him.

Michael complained about his bowels and insufficient amount of toilet paper he receives each week. "Did you tell the doctor about your problems?" I asked. "Maybe you could get a colonoscopy or a lower GI?" I suggested. Michael shrugged and didn't say anything. Later, I asked my mother if he was getting appropriate medical care.

"He doesn't want to be anesthetized during the procedure," she said. Not that I could blame him. The State of Ohio had been previously seeking the death penalty against my brother. While Michael suffers from paranoia, even a rational person who had been through that would resist being put under, even for benign purposes. "He doesn't want to lose control of his body for any period of time," my mother continued. "He refused to give blood for a DNA sample after he was arrested. He thought they might try to clone him."

After John and I returned from Toledo, I got an email from C.P.: *Hey, you missed the post-reunion parties. I went to one at Liz's house. Amy, Susan, Shannon and Brian were there. The conversation mostly was about politics—and only one Republican in the group...*

The short email left me devastated. I should have gone to the party, but I had been too terrified. Here I am, confronted by my own lameness. I see myself damaged, calculating the price of emotionally isolating myself from all but a few. I should have felt at home, welcomed in a place where people know me and love me and think I am smart and funny and kind. Unwittingly, I had left the girl I used to be behind. As long as I carry the guilt my brother cannot feel, there is no harbor, no soft and gentle resting place, where I can ask for forgiveness for a crime I did not commit.

"You are making assumptions about people and you don't even know if they are true," John said. "You are assuming they will give you the worst, and you have never asked."

I don't want to know. I want to go back to Seattle. I love Seattle, and I don't know why. I have friends, but not the crowd I had in Ohio or the wide circle I had in Chicago. Seattle is full of transplants, like me, who have lived so many places, they don't know where to call home. Seattle is cool, like London or San Fran; not fashionable like New York or Los Angeles. Unlike in other parts of the country, most people here don't care what car they drive or how fancy their house is. It is also the land of *don't ask, don't tell.* The women at my daughter's bus stop asked about my brother once and I said he was institutionalized with schizophrenia. I didn't mention what kind of institution, and nothing more was asked.

Sometimes I wish I could be out about my brother, tell the world and divide it into those who are sympathetic to the tragedy and those who are only repulsed. I think about moving back to Ohio, where my parents could watch my kids on weekends and I could hang out with Elizabeth. I think of the moving truck pulling up to my new home, the neighbors coming out, eventually asking "Are you related to…" and then I stop. I drift off in the temperate climate of the Pacific Northwest, sitting on the beach with the Olympic Mountains on the horizon while my preschool age son digs in the sand, diverting a creek to the Puget Sound.

Flower Fetish

By Michael Boudreaux

MOST OBSESSIVES FIXATE ON SOMETHING they can either consume or collect, probably research extensively, search out, and ultimately waste precious free time focused on that one thing, the object of their obsession. I have been obsessed with good wine, booze of different types. There was the specialty gin period, single malt scotches before that. At one point I was particularly fond of small vintage Calvados from family farms in Normandy. I have dabbled in good food: name a cuisine and I am sure I will have spent time there singularly focused. Travel, books, Pez dispensers, all pretty standard, garden variety fixations. It wasn't until I moved to a farm that things got a bit more perverse. My garden-variety obsession went to the next level. I discovered the devil's flower, dahlias.

I had never liked dahlias. They always seemed too contrived, too ostentatious, too something. Like inbred show dogs, dahlias struck me as neurotic. I had no interest in these prissy, clown-like flowers. I carefully avoided them at garden centers and in spring catalogues. Such was their sway over me early on.

My descent down that slippery slope began at a co-worker's house party. I was fairly new to the area and had just bought a small house with acreage in rural King County. In an effort to be more social, I forced myself to attend these Friday, after work get-togethers. These pseudo- corporate gatherings were a good way to network, get the scoop on what was really happening at work and avoid drinking alone. Mainly though, the focus would be alcohol. Endless talk about work, after working all week, always seemed tedious. I would feign interest in the triumphs and pitfalls of the latest project, endure the endless gossip and office intrigues.

Up until this point I had lived, so I thought, an adventure-filled life: traipsing through the jungles of Paraguay, helping set up public health programs in Central America and for a while living the contemplative life as a Trappist monk high up in the Rocky Mountains. An inexplicable turn of events in my life had led me somewhat dejectedly back to a mind-numbing biotech job in Bothell, Washington and with it, an endless string of boring after work parties in Seattle suburbs.

One particular night, realizing I couldn't possibly consume enough gin and tonics to remotely call it a fun party, I wandered outside and caught up with a group of women touring the garden in the fading light. The happy couple was growing, of all things, dahlias. Yawn. The wife blathered on as I distractedly peered through their neighbor's window. The blue glow of the TV was flashing images from ESPN. In the darkened living room I could see two muscular, hairy legs on a coffee table next to several empty beer bottles. The garden tour meandered on below the fence line, and I never got to see the face of the boxer-clad neighbor who owned those beefy gams. The wife asked me if I knew this one. I tried to refocus on the dahlias and was amazed to see, what I later learned was a collaret dahlia name *Little Showoff*.

"This is a dahlia?" I asked incredulously.

"If you like it I can give you a piece. We divided them earlier this spring. I might have some left," she responded with the voice of a temptress. I should have known: the first one is always free.

Before leaving that night, the wife took me to the garage and gave me a few tubers of *Little Showoff*. Piles of other tubers were laid out on newspaper. "You can't just take *one*. Let's see what we have left." She started looking at the tags. "*Jennifer Lynn* is a beauty. And this one, *Juanita*, is really sweet, dark purple." She started handing me clumps of tubers. I tried to protest, but I am weak when it comes to resisting free things. The numerous gin and tonics helped erode my resolve. Somewhere in the back of my mind I knew this dahlia thing could become a problem. I had known crazed dahlia people in Toronto.

"*Thomas Edison*," she continued, "is a classic, big solid flowers. And this is a good one," she said breaking off another clump. "It's a big white flowered one called *Gitts Attention*. Very appropriately named," she said, looking back at me over the top of her glasses. She rooted around through the piles until she picked up a lone tuber with writing on it. She held it to her heart. "You *must* have this one. He's a very big boy." She made a very Earth Kitt-esque cat sound. "*Spartacus.* Wow. This is an amazing flower. Big and full, virile, dark crimson…" I thought she was going to swoon.

"Seriously, this is more than enough," I protested. "Thanks so much."

I drifted off into the night with my grocery bag full of dahlia tubers, unaware that I had just begun my descent into dahlia madness.

The easy cultivation and instant gratification of these dramatic flowers, along with a little money I made from my pathetic roadside stand, helped change my opinions towards these neurotic show dogs. It wasn't long before the likes of *April Dawn, Lydia Suckow* and *Gay Princess* made their way to my flower beds. There were countless others that soon followed, *Akita No Hikari, Bodacious,* and *Kidd's Climax* among them. I started frequenting spring dahlia sales. I sought out the rare, the obscure and the magnificent online. I'd get giddy as my credit card got more use than it should have. I couldn't get enough.

I went to Dahlia Society meetings. I learned that dahlias were promiscuous breeders. This didn't seem to scandalize the blue rinse geezers in the audience. Titillated, I soon found myself hybridizing dahlias, playing out Gregor Mendel fantasies from my quasi monastic perch in Carnation. My own crosses began producing as I systematically named and catalogued them.

During one marathon spending spree online I realized I was sliding down that slippery slope. The new acquisitions continued with names like; *Inflammation, Sugar Lips, Pee Wee Colonel* and *Junkyard Dog.* This last one was an expensive disappointment but a genius of marketing.

It soon became apparent my rototiller could no longer keep up with the pace of growth. My neighbor began plowing and disking my field with his tractor as my garden quickly became a farm. Summers became an outrageous orgy of color and saturnalian cross-pollination. With it came endless staking and dead-heading, followed by the flopping mildew of fall and ultimately the tedious, back breaking winter tuber digging, which included cleaning, labeling and storing.

I soon found myself planting more flowers than I could ever possibly deal with. A friend of mine asked at one point as we looked out to a sea of flowers from my back deck, "What are you going to do with all of these?"

"I don't know." It was a question I should have been asking myself for quite some time.

I had vague ideas of internet tuber sales, expanding the cut flower sales but honestly this dahlia thing was getting out of hand. I could finally see it from my friend's perspective. I had a problem. Realizing this could have been the first step on the path to recovery. St Augustine came to mind, "Give me chastity and continence, but not yet." I wanted to be free of this compulsion but I wasn't ready, not yet.

I began to recruit friends, co-workers and people I barely knew into this adventure. Even so, I realized there would never be enough time or energy to deal with all that I had planted. I continued finding cultivars that I didn't possess and, ashamedly, still felt compelled to obtain; *Stephen David, Taboo, Maniac.* Many of my seedlings showed promise which meant I would carry them forward for another year. All of this added more work, requiring more storage space each winter. Mentally I tried to downsize. When it came to actually letting marginal cultivars rot, I found it hard to let go. More often than not I could find something positive in a mediocre cross to save it from the compost heap. Thankfully some attrition occurred due to natural causes. Some tubers never came back. Every year there was net gain, not loss. More, more, more.

As another dahlia-filled season came to an end, I counted nearly 300 named cultivars, often in multiples, and another 200 or so seedlings from my crosses. Each one formed huge, heavy wet clumps of tubers that would have to be dug up, washed, labeled, stored and eventually divided in spring.

As it did every year, the day I decided to dig tubers it would rain and threaten to flood or snow or both. The friends I would enlist to help were usually busy or suddenly sick on that freezing wet Saturday the annual event took place. One winter evening, long after an old lady friend had gone home (the only one who had showed up to help), I stood shivering in the falling snow. My hands and feet were frostbitten from digging all day in the wet cold. My back ached. I found myself near tears, angry at my own stupidity as I dipped another heavy clump of tubers into the bleach bath. I was exhausted. This dahlia thing had gotten away from me. I needed help.

The next spring I approached the "dahlia situation" with strong determination. There were several cultivars that I had to admit, were boring, and would no longer be joining their compatriots in the field. After my paltry tuber sales at the farm, I gave away bags of dahlias to anyone who showed even remote interest, free. Still, I had a net gain of forty-three dahlia cultivars from the previous year.

Every time I looked out to the sea of dahlias, all I saw was an endless ocean of unfinished work and responsibility. Having spent time in a monastic setting contemplating my true nature, I realized I had little control over my impulses. (Isn't the first of the twelve steps realizing you are powerless in the face of your addiction?) Reluctant to use up precious prayer points for something lame like dahlia discernment, I still found myself praying for guidance. I needed to find a way out of the maze these self-inflicted, endless rows of dahlias had created.

Be careful what you ask for.

My usual manic spring enthusiasm had waned that next year. I couldn't tell if I was losing interest in dahlias, was overwhelmed or I was simply getting older. I cut back on the dead-heading and did much less staking than in years previous. By late August it was a beautiful but overgrown mess. In late September I decided that I would only save the top 100 cultivars and let the rest rot in the field. I carefully tagged all the dahlias I was going to keep. By the time Barack Obama was elected to office, the dahlias were still flowering. The tubers were nowhere near ready for digging. This was the beginning of a bad flood year in the Snoqualmie valley.

The first flood came a few days after the election as I attended a conference in Aspen. I was ecstatic the Bush era was finally behind us. I called my partner, Daniel, at home and found out the fields were flooding, still green with dahlias. The dahlias had been through floods before so I knew it wouldn't kill them. Soaking in saturated mud would definitely weaken them. I would have to dig them up as soon as I got home.

At home, on another predictably cold and shitty day digging dahlias, I was proud of myself. I actually did let go of several hundred dahlias. I still dug up more than my planned allotment of 100, but it was a start. They began drying on the basement floor just as the second flood of the year began to make its way down the valley. We were used to floods, but it was rare to get water in the basement. By the time the flood prediction came, it was clear the dahlias would be underwater. We had little time to save the equipment, tools, gear and everything else that we stored down there. The dahlias would have to endure another soaking. Water was lapping at the doorway by the time we removed the last of the bikes and power tools.

The flood was much higher than predicted. We heard things tipping over in the middle of the night, metal clangs and water splashing in the rising floodwater. When it crested we had nearly four feet of water in the basement, the worst flood we had been through. The clean-up was depressing just before the holidays. Silt covered every surface the water touched. We pulled out everything remaining on the floor, hosed the basement out and dried it with fans and heaters. I halfway expected the dahlias to be mushy with rot, but they were solid and seemingly unscathed. Wistfully, I read the tags as I laid them back on the newly dried floor; *Kasasagi, Urchin, Swan's Sunset.* All of them unique beauties I wasn't ready to let go of.

After the holidays, we looked forward to the promise of a new year, even as the economy was tanking. We were grateful to both be healthy, still employed, and for the most part, happy. But, seven days into the new year we found ourselves in serious trouble. NOAA and the Northwest River Forecast started putting out cryptic warnings that were so absurd they almost seemed like a joke. Things like: "possibility of two feet of rain in the mountains on four feet of fresh snow." "Disastrous, record high flood levels." "sixty feet of water at Carnation." (Flood level is fifty-four feet.)

We began to scramble, moving everything back out of the basement and up onto the deck. We had just been through two big floods that season and were overwhelmed having to face possibly the worst flood on record.

We figured out where a sixty-foot flood would rise to in our basement and took everything out below that level. As water once again began lapping at the basement door, everything was up, dahlias included.

Daniel and I sat down to a glass of wine as the waters quickly rose. We were exhausted and anxious, though glad that everything was up out of harm's way. As the storm developed we had surprisingly little rain in the valley. Unknown to us, the sky was falling in the mountains. We watched in horror as water quickly crept up the walls of our house and drowned all the familiar landmarks in our yard. The street in front of our house became a rushing torrent that eventually reached a height of eight feet deep. The crushing force and volume was unfathomable. My worst fear was that a log would crash into the side of the house and knock it off the foundation. Strange that would even be something one could fear.

Since our house is raised we never really fear water getting inside the living space. Regardless, it is always nerve wracking. As the flood reached the predicted crest, it continued rising. In the darkness outside we sat on the porch, a few inches above the murky floodwater. Strange noises filled the night along with the ever present rushing water. At one point the mewling of a cow in trouble slowly drifted by in the distance. We could only assume the worst. Odd objects floated by with amazing speed. Plastic buckets, logs, pumpkins, even a Styrofoam head.

Later, Daniel woke me around 4am to say water was coming over the top of the driveway. Water had begun covering the dahlias.

By daylight, the floodwaters had finally crested at 62.2 feet, the worst flood on record and more than two feet above the line we had evacuated to in the basement. The basement was filled with seven feet of silty floodwater. The dahlias were completely submerged as water flowed across the driveway. I realized maybe my discernment was at hand. I regretted not setting aside some of my crosses that no one else had or ever would again. But, the dahlias, at the moment, were the least of my worries.

You know it's bad when the Red Cross shows up at your house. Daniel and I were already hauling the remains of our silt covered things from the basement when they pulled up. Numb from the trauma we had just gone through, it was a shock to see it from a stranger's eyes. I told the woman in the Red Cross vehicle that where her car was parked there had been 8 feet of rushing water. I pointed to the debris hanging from the trees. The awe on her face never left, even as she told us there was nothing they could do to help. We trudged on salvaging what we could, purging what we couldn't.

As if this hadn't been too much already, it snowed 3 days later, followed by a hard freeze. The remaining dahlias were still sitting on the driveway unprotected. I stood there in the snow and felt a rush of relief. Whether I was ready for it or not, I was done with dahlias. What

I hadn't been able to do on my own had been done for me. I did feel a twinge of withdrawal. *Bracken Ballerina, Citron du Cap* or *Hillcrest Kismet* would no more brighten my summers.

Back inside the house, next to the warm fire I popped open my laptop and idly surfed. I didn't want to think about the mess on the driveway I would eventually have to haul off into the woods. Checking email, there was already a note from one of the dahlia wholesalers with pre-season offers. I started to delete it but opened it instead, for old time's sake. There was nothing new or compelling with their dahlias. They also sold daylilies. Perusing their catalog I found some amazing daylily cultivars I'd never seen; *Barbarian Princess, Lord of the Storm, Space Coast Cotton Candy*. Before I knew it, I was typing in my credit card number.

Maybe coming down off dahlias wasn't going to be *that* painful.

Choosing Mastectomy

By Wendy Staley Colbert

I HAVE A COMPLEX RELATIONSHIP WITH CANCER. I abhor it and I welcome it. My grandmother got cancer in her 40s and it killed her. My mom got cancer in her 40s and it transformed her. She always loved life, but after her diagnosis, she fully embraced it; petty grievances like traffic jams failed to irk her, and even grand grievances like deaths in the family were tolerable.

Now, at 43, tiny dots of cancer cells had been detected behind my right nipple. I had a decision to make: lumpectomy and radiation or mastectomy. The choice was mine.

Because of my family history, you could say I expected cancer when it came knocking on my door. I pulled over to the side of the road when my oncology surgeon called after the biopsy. She uttered a bunch of clinical phrases that I frantically scribbled on scrap paper —Ductal Carcinoma In Situ, stage 0, genetic testing recommended, more surgery necessary - but the word 'malignant' rung in my ear like destiny echoing through the decades. As I hung up the phone, tears filled my eyes and dribbled down my cheeks. For twenty-some years, since my mother's own diagnosis, a part of me had expected this call, had anticipated and already begun to grieve. I was now linked to Grandma Clara, who I never got to meet. Clara's doctor didn't give her a diagnosis—by the time they caught hers, it had metastasized and was terminal. Clara died too young, without choices, barely even knowing what she had.

My mom had choices. When she found a lump at forty-seven, she chose to remove it, and save her breast by irradiating it.

As the third generation, I felt anxious about making the right choice. Immediately after getting the diagnosis, I felt sorry for myself. I didn't want to have to do anything. I dealt with my anxiety by gathering information—researching treatment options on the internet, talking with other patients, and interviewing doctors. Over the next four weeks, I became well-versed in BRCA gene mutations, the likelihood of recurrence, the long-term side effects of radiation, and the breast reconstruction process. I wanted to make the choice that would give me the best odds of long-term health and that would cause as few adverse effects as possible. I asked myself: Which choice would I make if I viewed my breasts practically as optional body parts, similar to the appendix? What if I could trust that my self-image would remain intact no matter how my appearance was altered? Was my self-worth greater than the sum of individual body parts? The more information I gathered, and the more I fished the depths of my psyche, the more apparent my preferred choice became.

I chose bilateral mastectomy. Let the transformation begin.

I bought two zip-up sweat jackets to wear in the days following my mastectomy. Pain, numbness and limited range of motion make it difficult to raise your arms to put on a blouse. Plus, it's helpful to have inside pockets to hold the plastic bulb that dangles from the drainage tube emerging from each of your sides and fills up with a mixture of yellowish fluids and blood suctioned from inside your chest.

I selected fleecy sweat jackets—one a practical gray and one the color of a barely ripened strawberry. When I was 5, my favorite jacket was the same style and light-red color, hooded with twin blue stripes encircling the wrist bands. I wore that jacket every spring day my kindergarten year, and loved it so much my mom sewed individual navy-blue capital letters on the part that rested on the nape of my neck—'W"E"N"D"Y'. I treasured it like a teddy bear – it was a reminder of the warmth and coziness of home, when I was far from it in my classroom.

The day after the surgery when it was time to get ready to return home, I decided to wear the red one, and changed into it with the help of my husband in the toilet area of the hospital room—an area with no mirror.

I rested my fingers on the bend of his arm to steady myself, and avoided looking down at my chest by fixing my gaze on the translucent sliding door behind him. As Mark gently slipped off the gown, I felt a combination of loss and triumph. I realized part of me was forever gone, but also that the toughest ordeal—the surgery to remove my breasts—was over. I felt reassured, remembering Mark's reaction after I had told him of my decision to have a mastectomy a few weeks earlier. "I love you with or without breasts," he had said. Now I watched for changes in his expression as he slid a fleecy sleeve up each of my arms, and slowly zipped up the front. I had minimal pain, but still felt groggy from the after-effects of the anesthesia. To my relief, his face registered only calm caring, not the repulsion a part of me had feared. Earlier that morning, my doctor had matter-of-factly unsnapped the top of my hospital gown to check the incisions on my chest, and said, "Looks good. Different, I know." I had met her eyes and smiled, but barely glanced down. I didn't feel ready yet to see the full effects of the surgery.

When I got home, I was instructed not to shower for the first few days. I was pleased, because it meant I could continue cloaking my new appearance for awhile. My sweat jacket lay amazingly flat against my chest, reminding me of when I was a prepubescent child. I'd unzip the sweat jacket and open one side like a magician revealing the inside of his cape, so that my husband could empty out that drainage bulb, then open the other side so the same could be done. It was a nauseating exercise, because of the yellowish-red color of the fluid, the slurping sound, and the feeling of the strong suction deep near my ribs. I gulped down lumps in my throat as Mark carefully measured the volume of fluid being expressed each day. I was impressed that he seemed less revolted than I was. To distract ourselves during the process, we joked about the 'zing' he caused me to feel when he got really good suction, and commented on how well I seemed to be healing.

I focused the first few days on resting and recovery from the surgery itself, and put off confronting my new body. I imagined how my best self would handle this change, and I tried to act like that person—serene and accepting. I felt a tenderness toward myself I had never before experienced. I remembered feeling loved as a child, before I had breasts. Most of all, I worked on keeping this challenge in perspective. I wasn't my grandma, whose cancer had been detected at a more advanced stage, who didn't get to choose her course of treatment. I wouldn't require the hardship of chemotherapy; I wasn't truly fighting for my life.

I was adjusting to a new reality, though, and accepting a new vulnerability. In some ways, I felt my body had let me down. I could no longer rely on the naïve illusion of perfect health as I aged. I began to get used to this altered self, internally and externally. Through the process of emptying the drainage bulbs in the first days of recovery, I snuck peeks at my chest—one small eyeful at a time. I got slowly acquainted with my new appearance as if it was a lover, through stolen glances here and there. Finally, it was time to take a shower and wash my own hair, and I felt ready to fully unveil.

I unzipped, removed one arm and then the other, shaking the warmth of the sweat jacket to the cold, hard tiles of the bathroom floor. I stood before the mirror completely exposed. A 4-inch strip of surgical tape ran on top of each horizontal incision, and underneath I could see gathers and folds of skin, like a beginner seamstress had given a set of curtains or pleated skirt waistline her best shot. All the tissue was gone, as were the nipples. I didn't realize how far breast tissue extended into the upper chest and under the arm. These areas were indented now—concave where my eye expected to see bounty – a rise or a bulge. But my skin remained. It was a comfort to see the mole right where it should be on my upper left chest.

I raised my gaze to meet my own eyes in the mirror, and gave my reflection the shyest of smiles. It wasn't ugly. I saw the whole me—the girl, the woman I used to be, and now the survivor. I saw me. And I was beautiful.

About six weeks after the mastectomy, I entered through a doorway on the second floor of the Seattle Art Museum. A shimmering metal robe with bell-shaped sleeves, like a kimono, towered before me. It was seemingly free-standing with no visible support except the metal pieces themselves. The glints of the rounded, rectangular silver shapes started at the shoulders and continued overlapping, spilling into a generous train that formed a semi-circle on the gleaming hardwood floor. I approached and stood inches away from it to get a better look at the detail. On closer inspection, I found that each metal piece was imprinted with typeface. I felt confused. I turned away to read the descriptive panel mounted on a nearby wall, and it all became clear.

Each of the 40,000 metal pieces was a dog tag, like those worn by military personnel.

In that moment, my perception of the robe changed. The garment became heartbreakingly beautiful. The outer beauty apparent to the eye had fused with the meaning that only became apparent on close inspection. The greatest beauty comes from depth, comes from an understnding that is not easily achieved, but is earned. It's this complexity and the never-ending layers of meaning that give richness to our perception of an object or a person. You have to work at it to fully appreciate it. I call it transformation.

Midpoint

By Heather Patrick

IT HAPPENED WITHOUT WARNING OR OBVIOUS CAUSE. It happened so fast and was so complete an experience, I neither feared nor doubted its veracity. Six years later, I am still grappling with the enormity of what it meant.

My husband and I were halfway through a six-year adventure, sailing from Seattle to New Zealand. We were anchored inside the lagoon on Huihini, a quiet atoll in French Polynesia north of the more touristy islands of Moorea and Tahiti. I was sitting on the bow of our boat, enjoying the gorgeous South Pacific day: bright sun sparkling on turquoise water, trade winds rustling the nearby palm trees and carrying the scent of plumeria flowers and ripe papaya out to the boat.

And then all of that was gone and I was standing, as if in a waking dream, at an intersection on a flat, barren piece of land out in the middle of nowhere. Everything was dry: the wind, the dust, my mouth. Straight ahead and to my right I saw nothing but desolate, empty land. I looked to my left and instantly everything shifted, like that cinematography effect when the actor is propelled forward toward the camera while the background recedes and then resets at a distance, slightly out of focus.

And in that moment, I understood that I had just reached middle-age and was looking at the second half my life. I was forty-three. Behind me, the road that had brought me to this place vanished; there would be no returning to youth. I looked down the course remaining and saw near the horizon, for the first time, the end of the road.

And just that fast I was back, sitting on the bow, savoring the moist, tropical air and trying to make sense of what had just happened. I remembered that both my maternal grandmother and great-grandmother had died at eighty-six. Had the universe just told me I had exactly 43 years left? On that perfect South Pacific day, the thought felt abstract, the end date far away.

Some years earlier, I had had a similar experience after my dad died. It was during my first ocean crossing, an all-woman's training course sailing from Hawaii to San Juan Island in Washington. I had just finished a night watch with my team of crewmates and was climbing into my berth for a few hours of sleep before our next turn at the wheel. At the moment I put my head on the pillow, I was standing at the outskirts of a small town. It appeared to be circa 1940s with sturdy old brick buildings from the late 19th century, a few dirt roads, a few old trucks, and grass growing wild in a vacant lot. It was late afternoon; I remember the town smelled warm, as if the ground, buildings, and trees had absorbed a summer's worth of sun and could no longer contain the heat.

I wandered through town until I heard voices and decided to follow the sound. As I got closer, I saw my Dad sitting with a gang of cronies on old folding chairs in someone's backyard. Men in boots, jeans, and flannel shirts, some skinny, some like my Dad with big bellies ballooning out between suspenders, a drink in one hand and a cigar in the other. They were telling stories and laughing.

When my Dad saw me, his face lit up; he jumped out of his chair, hugged me and said, "I'm so glad you've come." He introduced to me to his friends as he had in life, "This is my star." After a round of enthusiastic greetings, Dad said, "I'll show you around." We walked through town, and he pointed out his favorite diner and the shop where one of his "lady friends" worked. I smiled to see him so happy, so much in his element. And at the very moment I realized I was in my Dad's heaven, I was back in my berth in the middle of the Pacific Ocean. I opened my eyes and was bathed in a rush of warmth that smelled like late summer sunshine.

I don't know if it was an out-of-body phenomenon, or if I had fallen asleep and it was a dream. But I know that I visited Dad in his heaven. It's the same primal certainty I felt when I stood at the crossroads and knew I had reached midlife.

Nothing drastic or immediate happened as a result of realizing I was officially middle-aged. I didn't feel or look any different. In fact, in spite of being perpetually overweight, I felt pretty buff! I was swimming almost daily, hiking around islands, and raising fifty-pound anchors and large canvas sails on a regular basis. Wasn't forty the new thirty for my generation?

But below the surface, the tectonic plates of my existence were shifting. Middle-age was pushing to the surface, infiltrating my thoughts, changing my body, and messing with my expectations. I remember the first time I thought, "No one will ever describe me again as a young woman"; it was an odd and indisputable new truth. And then there's the new habit of standing in front of a mirror, pulling at the skin on my face, and imagining what a little "work" could do for me. I remember, in my early twenties, declaring emphatically to my young and equally fresh-faced friends, "I would never consider plastic surgery; women should embrace the changes to their appearance." Ha!

When I was 44, I was on a hike in New Zealand and fell into a fence-post hole; both my knees slammed hard into a rough concrete slab. This stunned me more than anything, and before I even worried about my knees, I spent a good few minutes cursing the person who had neglected to fill the hole. My knees were bleeding a bit but still worked, as they always had, and so I walked another couple of miles, climbed up through a small ravine, and made my way back to our boat.

Five years later, while climbing the stairs at my health club, I am reminded for the umpteenth time that my midlife fall caused the first injury from which I have never completely healed. As I make my slow progression up the stairs, deliberately taking one plodding step at a time to keep my knees from protesting with pain, men and women with younger, healthier bodies, dart, leap, and surge past me. I feel like a large stone in the middle of a river, slowly eroding while the water rushes past.

It's not that middle-age is ALL about deterioration; I have also felt shifts in perspective that allow me to be less defensive, to accept my imperfections with a bit more grace, and to let go of *some* of the things I can't control. But with so many changes, I find myself feeling about middle-age the way Alice felt about Wonderland: "Curiouser and curiouser."

What I hadn't expected about middle-age was that my youthful expectations would simply no longer apply. That my way of moving through the world, both physically and emotionally, would change. That beyond the discomfort of menopause, age spots, and injuries that don't heal, I would begin to understand that my life is, in fact, finite.

Until reaching midlife, mortality had always been a philosophical topic at dinner parties, not a visceral reality that I understood in my bones. I was thirty-five before anyone close to me died. When my grandmother died at eighty-six, her death seemed reasonable, natural. My dad died unexpectedly at sixty-five, but he was overweight, drank too much, and didn't exercise. It's not that these deaths weren't painful; they were just somehow disconnected from my age. I still had the arrogant expectation of youth: that my life was defined by endless horizons and opportunities. My mantra was, "I'll do *this* now, because I can always do *that* later."

This all changed when Scott, my oldest brother, was diagnosed with terminal brain cancer at the age of 48 and died two and a half years later. Suddenly mortality is everywhere. I hear it in the voices of my friends telling me about researching retirement communities for their parents; it hangs in the air like a shoe waiting to drop when yet another phone call starts with "I have bad news;" it shadows the profound urgency with which I now look at my life, my marriage, my choices.

As I continue to age, I find myself remembering with increasing frequency my visit to the midlife crossroads. And while it has taken a while to sink in, seeing the remaining years of my life contained has caused me to acknowledge that I don't want the second half of my life to be a mirror image of the first. I want the second half of my life to be on my terms. But the distance between acknowledgment and action is proving to be as vast and barren as the crossroads that got me here.

In his writings about "The Hero's Journey," Joseph Campbell defined a classic sequence of actions that have been found in human stories for centuries: a call to adventure, a road of trials, achieving the goal or boon, returning to the ordinary world, and applying the boon for the greater good. And while this never happens in the movies, the whole process can actually end at the first step if the hero refuses the call. That's where I am: deciding *should I stay or should I go?*

Even with my new middle-age mantra, "If not now, when?" playing in my head, I struggle with rewiring myself. When I say I want the second half of my life to be on my terms, I mean that I want to be more self-determining. I want to make my happiness my priority. My life feels too defined by other people's needs. But to make these changes, my road of trials may very well include leaving my marriage, giving up the protection of being overweight, and moving beyond not only the loss of my brother, but the loss of my surviving family as I knew it before Scott died.

And according to Campbell, I can fail at any point.

So why go? Why take the leap? I love my husband and he loves me—we are each other's "person." But after fifteen years, our differences are outweighing what has held us together, and we seem incapable of stopping the progression. We could easily stay together, but at what cost?

And at what cost is the extra sixty pounds I carry on my 5'4" frame? Since I was a girl, my weight has been a manifestation of trying to suppress emotions. Oh sure, I love food and I am not a disciplined person, but the reality is my weight makes me feel safe. Giving it up is not just a matter of diet and exercise; I only know myself as a fat person. But I'm approaching fifty, and this monkey has been on my back too long.

And then there is the shifting dynamic of my family. When my brother was diagnosed with brain cancer, my family rose to the occasion as if on wings of grace. Without exception, we became the best versions of ourselves: generous, loving, supportive, caring. Scott's caregivers and friends even commented on our astonishing unity, good humor, and commitment. But that all dissolved into the vacuum of grief that was left by Scott's death. With our focal point gone, some of us retreated while others grew angry and lashed out. I had expected the waves of grief that washed over me at the loss of my brother, but the wave that knocked me down and threatened to drown me was the loss of my family.

Recently I asked myself: "What do you want? Separate from what anybody else in your life wants, *what do you want?*" And my mind formed an immediate and clear answer. "I want to be happier than I am sad. I want to be more joyful than I am angry. I want to live my life without fear. And I want something big to look forward to; something I can work toward and make happen."

And with this statement I realize, that like my visit to Dad's heaven and my midlife crossroads, I have received another gift. What I want, I have had before. It is my essential way of being. My truest, best form. Over the past few years, I've lost sight of it. My call to adventure is to reclaim it. My call to adventure is to reclaim myself.

Wallflowers Don't Always Triumph
at the High School Reunion
by Christiane Banta

I HATED HIGH SCHOOL. I WASN'T AT ALL POPULAR, and I wasn't athletic. I was a good student, but most of my classmates were too, in the affluent suburb where I lived. My family was poor, I was shy, and I wasn't pretty. I wasn't artsy or had anything else that set me apart, that protected me against the pain of not being popular.

My thirty-year reunion wasn't well timed for me to show off how well I had succeeded in life. A couple of years before, I had been laid off after a year-long medical leave of absence for breast cancer. I had moved into an apartment in my basement and rented out the rest of my house to cut my expenses. Then I had a recurrence. A year and a half later, treatments completed and my savings exhausted, I went back to work. But I was still living in my basement. Oh, and I had never married and had no children.

Believe it or not, this stuff didn't matter to me. I was happy with the way things had turned out with my life and I considered myself very lucky. I had recovered my health, still had my house and retirement savings, and was in the best romantic relationship of my life, with a guy who had been there for me through everything.

I wasn't planning to attend the 30-year reunion. In fact, I wasn't even invited. For the 10th and 20th year reunions the invitations had included my name on the list of graduates with address unknown, but on the 30th I had been dropped altogether. This was fine with me; I didn't care about anyone but my friends, and I was still in touch with them. But those friends decided to go to the reunion, and to have dinner together before. The last time we had all been together was our senior year at that very high school, so I went along.

My friends and I had a wonderful time at dinner. Afterwards, as we walked the short distance from the restaurant to the reunion, I felt like I was regressing to high school and was on my way to a dance, where I would stand alone all evening, feeling like an idiot. I didn't care about the people at the reunion—why was I going? But I reassured myself that a lot of time had passed; we weren't the same insensitive kids we used to be. And, if I was having a lousy time, I could just leave, and never see them again.

The party was held in a billiard hall in another affluent suburb not very different from my home town. The billiard hall was a bad choice. It was hard for groups to gather in the small spaces between the tables, and there were no chairs.

After a time my friends wandered off to talk to other people. I saw Dianne, someone I remembered from high school, and went over to say hello. Her hair style and color, her makeup, and her conservative style of clothes were unchanged. I would have recognized her anywhere.

"Hi, Dianne," I said, happy to be able to talk to someone I remembered. "Tell me about your life in the last thirty years."

Dianne scowled at me. "I married, had a daughter now in college and a son in high school, and my husband told me a month ago that after twenty-four years of marriage he wants out."

"I'm so sorry," I said. I wanted to be nice to her. I seemed to remember we hadn't always been nice to each other in high school.

"The thing is, he's sick. He's really sick. He's so sick he needs someone to care for him. He might even die. But now he doesn't want me around, not even to take care of him. And what's worse, there isn't anyone else. He left me because he doesn't want to be with me, even when he's sick."

Twenty minutes later, Dianne was still talking. Her job didn't pay enough for her to continue living in the suburb where we had grown up. Her daughter had sided with her husband in the separation, but she was doing her best to turn their son against his father.

I was beginning to feel sympathy for her husband who had stayed with her an incomprehensible twenty-four years. I was also pleased that my dislike of her in high school seemed to show good judgment on my part.

"Oh well," Dianne said finally, with a sigh and a smile. "I guess I shouldn't be so negative. At least we have our health, right?"

I hesitated. I hadn't been planning to talk about myself, but couldn't resist a set up line like that.

"Actually," I said, "I just finished a year of treatments for a recurrence of breast cancer."

Dianne stared at me, her eyes wide. There was a long silence as I waited, curious, for her reaction.

"My husband is really sick, too," she said finally, and started what appeared to be another lengthy rant on the theme of her own suffering.

I was done with her. I had listened to her long enough and obviously she wouldn't, or maybe she couldn't, reciprocate.

"I see," I said. I started backing away from her. "I'm going …" I turned as I mumbled, "over there." I didn't care if she thought I was rude.

***

There's a school of thought that getting cancer is a wake-up call, an opportunity to reevaluate and make changes that you need to make, literally to save your life. This wasn't true for me. I had done a thorough evaluation of my life right before getting cancer, and had already made those changes.

That evaluation happened when I was forty years old. I had taken a job that had consumed all my time, and given me chronic insomnia. As I lay awake each night, I thought. I thought about my life, my career, my past, my future. Everything.

Had I made a mistake in my career that had lead me to this job, and if so, what was it? What did I really want? What could I do to get what I really wanted? I thought about the men I had known. Why had I never married? How did I feel about not having children? Had I let my career overwhelm my personal life? Did I regret my choices?

I thought deeply about these questions, not allowing myself to come to any conclusions without examining every assumption I had. Finally I decided that I hadn't made a mistake in staying single because none of the men I had dated could have been a lasting partner for me. I thought about what it would take for me to be happy with one person for a whole lifetime.

Within months I left that job for one that was less stressful. I realized I already knew a man who might be a perfect fit for me – my friend Jim. I hadn't talked to him in over a year, but I called and invited him to lunch.

Jim and I started dating officially the same week I got my breast cancer diagnosis. I told him I would understand if he had changed his mind about going out with me, if he would rather just stay friends. I told him it would be unfair of me to expect him to be my support when our relationship was so new. He didn't want me be alone, he assured me. He said he wanted us to go through it together.

Jim was with me for everything, his hands holding mine, his warmth and love comforting me. He curled himself around me as we slept. Before Jim, I couldn't sleep if I was being touched.

***

Halfway across the billiard room I turned around to see Dianne standing alone where I left her, gaze unfocused and inward, apparently lost in her own thoughts. Everyone else was leaving her alone.

"Hi," said an unfamiliar man as I turned back. He was smiling at me, with a welcoming, friendly expression on his face. "I don't think I knew you in high school, did I? I'm Peter."

"I'm Chris," I said. "I don't remember you, either. But it has been 30 years. I hardly remember anybody." I smiled back at him.

I could picture what Peter had looked like. His short wavy hair was only beginning to gray, but in the late 1970s it would have been shoulder length, dark brown, and curly. He probably would have been pretty skinny back then, but thirty years later he still looked fit.

"That's a beautiful blouse you're wearing," Peter said, staring at my breasts. He was a few inches shorter than I was, so he could do this without looking completely ridiculous. "Is that a blouse? Or would you call it a shirt?" He continued to stare at my chest, pretending to be considering the proper name for what I was wearing.

"I think we can call it a blouse," I said, amused. The garment in question was made out of a modern miracle fabric that was a little clingy, while de-emphasizing my weight.

"Are you married? Or with someone?"

"I'm in a serious relationship," I said. I knew telling him about Jim would probably put an end to Peter's flirting. I wasn't interested in him, but I hoped he would continue talking to me. So far he was more fun than Dianne had been.

"Is he here tonight?"

"No," I said, with a laugh. "It would be torture for him and I didn't see any reason to put him through it." I smiled to myself thinking of Jim, who was probably already asleep. The bed would be warm and cozy when I squirmed in next to him later that night.

Peter nodded. "It's the same with me. It's better for all concerned if the wife stays home. Hey, do you want to get out of here? I rented a hotel room about a block away. We can be there in minutes."

I was horrified. My first reaction was to tell him he was a creep and a loser. But that impulse faded quickly as I realized that he had made a straight-forward offer that I could refuse just as straight-forwardly.

"I'm not interested, Peter," I said, my voice calm, and I gave him a small smile to show I wasn't mad at him.

"Okay," he said, and quickly moved off in search of another target. I was relieved to see him go, but disappointed to be standing alone again.

I wandered into a small room off the larger billiard room, where a television played nonstop videos of the young kids who would have had nothing to do with me 30 years before, engaged in activities I hadn't been invited to. The adult versions of those kids had gathered around the television, laughing together, reminiscing, ignoring everyone else.

I looked around for my high school crush, curious about him. He had been hugely popular, of course, but was nicer than the rest. At least he had met my eyes in the hall and said hello to me in class. I didn't see him.

I spotted John across the room. He still looked young and thin, his blond hair short and slightly graying. His casual cotton shirt and jeans appeared to have been starched and ironed, which I thought was a little weird. We certainly didn't iron our jeans when we were in high school.

John and I had taken three years of Honors Math classes together. I still tell a story about how my 9th grade Honors Algebra II teacher motivated me to excel, a story that John has a part in. After I received an 89 on my final exam, I told the teacher I was going to retake it, which I was allowed to do. I wanted an A in the class, which meant getting at least a 90.

The teacher laughed at me and called out across the room, "John, what did you get on the final?"

"93!" John yelled back to everyone in the class.

"And you think you can do better than your 89?" the teacher asked me, with a smirk.

I got a 98. And the satisfaction of showing the teacher he was wrong, not that he ever acknowledged it, of course.

John went on to be a class valedictorian and an executive at Microsoft. I read about him in *Business Week* magazine.

For a moment I considered joining his group of friends to say hello, to tell John that I had read about him. I pictured them refusing to notice me as I stood beside them, then staring at me with hostility as I spoke. I imagined him saying something short and dismissive after I had finished, followed by my embarrassed retreat.

Instead, I left the party.

***

As I drove to Jim's place I thought about Peter, and his invitation. I realized that despite having stared at my prosthesis for some time, he could not have known that under my blouse, in place of my right breast, I had a flat chest with a four inch scar.

When the cancer returned I had to have a mastectomy. I had decided against reconstruction, at least immediately. I was tired of surgery, of recovering from treatments, of taking medication. I had spent years thinking about my breast, and was ready for that to change.

If I had been interested in Peter's invitation, if I had wanted to have sex with him, I would have to tell him about the scar where my breast used to be. It would have been impossible to go to a hotel room, throw our clothes off, and fall into bed together. It would be too much of a shock to him not to warn him. He might change his mind. He might not want to see me naked.

I realized that anonymous sex was impossible. I could choose to talk, or not to talk, about my cancer, but my naked body told my story without words. I hadn't realized this before because of Jim. Since the moment I knew he was the perfect fit for me, I hadn't thought about being with anyone else.

We Came to Say

***

After my treatments for the recurrence ended I joined a support group for women who had just finished their own breast cancer treatments. The group therapy sessions were like classes, with each meeting having a theme: what would we do with our lives, who would we be. I expected we would form a special bond, that we would understand each other in ways no one else could.

One week was dedicated to talking about sexuality. We had all felt ugly at some time during our treatments. Chemotherapy made our hair fall out, not only from our heads but also our eyelashes, eyebrows, and pubic hair. Lack of exercise and the steroids they gave us with chemotherapy made many of us gain weight, including me. I stopped looking in mirrors, and only saw myself as reflected in the love I could see in Jim's eyes. Peter was the first man who had come on to me in the years since my first cancer diagnosis.

I told the group what Peter had said.

"You must have felt flattered," one woman said.

"No, that wasn't it at all," I said. How could I possibly be flattered when he apparently made the invitation because I was in a solid relationship, and my partner wasn't there? He probably made the same offer to dozens of women that night. I wanted them to understand how thinking about Peter's offer had made me realize something I hadn't before. I had never thought about how my body had been permanently changed, and how it might look to someone seeing it for the first time.

I tried to explain my realization that I would never be able to have anonymous sex. "My body tells my story," I told the group.

"I thought you were happy with Jim," one protested.

"What would Jim say?" another accused.

Wendy, the youngest and only single woman in the group, said, "I know exactly what you mean." The other women just didn't understand, and didn't want to hear it. I was so disappointed.

***

I told Jim about Peter the night I returned from the reunion.

"Hey," he said, his voice heavy with sleep, as I pulled up the covers and snuggled into bed next to him. "Did you have fun?"

"No, but it was nice to see my friends," I said. Then I laughed. "A guy named Peter hit on me."

"Did you accept?" Jim's voice seemed a little less sleepy.

"No, of course not, silly."

"Why not?"

I snorted in response.

"But that made me realize something I hadn't thought of before—I'm not capable of anonymous sex any more. I mean, with my mastectomy scar, I would have to give the poor guy some sort of warning, which means a whole long conversation about the cancer and everything."

Jim ran his large hand lightly over the scar on my chest. "How do you feel about that?"

"I wouldn't, anyway. It's just weird to realize that I can't."

"I don't even remember what you used to look like," he said with a yawn. "You're just you."

I kissed him, then turned to curve my back against his front. His arms wrapped around me. Within minutes I could hear his soft slow breathing and knew he had fallen back asleep. I did remember what I used to look like, but because I was with Jim I didn't care.

Living On

By Rosemary Orr

ROBIN DIED THE DAY AFTER MOTHER'S DAY. I thought my life should end there—on May 15, 2006. How could I live after his death, the death of my son, a child I sought to save and protect? He was only twenty-four, his life extinguished in a moment.

For several days before that Monday, my daughter had been visiting from California and we were a little family again—Becky and Robin and I. We were still missing Arthur, my husband and their father, who had died four years before. It was good to be together again, under the same roof, sharing meals and conversation and catching up with each other.

On that Monday morning I needed a ride to work so that Becky could have my car to drive to meet her college counselor.

Robin was in the kitchen when I came to make coffee.

"Hi, Robin; are you still up?" Robin seemed to be having trouble sleeping and that worried me.

"Yeah, I'll sleep during the day," he answered, and we decided he would drive me to work.

We got in the car—a mother and son, driving together…"Do you remember that you have an appointment with the counselor on Wednesday?" I asked Robin. " I'm sorry I can't be there this time because of work," I added, feeling guilty once again that work was keeping me from lending him support.

Robin's pale face tensed and his blue eyes were hard. If I had not needed to be at work, I would have asked him to sit and talk. I would have asked him how he felt about the addiction counselor and to talk more about what had happened to provoke the visit to talk to a counselor.

A week before, Robin had come from his downstairs bedroom sleepy but very agitated.

"What day is it Mom? What time is it?"

I answered, and then really concerned, I made him sit with me on the sofa holding his long, slender body. He relaxed and calmed a little.

"What did you do last night? Did you use cocaine?"

I don't know why I asked that—perhaps the question was prompted by a buried intuition or old knowledge. I had been so worried about Robin's suspected drug use. His recent strange behavior, the daytime sleeping, isolating in his downstairs room and his pallor and weight loss made me wonder if he was using OxyContin® again. He had admitted to a problem months before and had agreed to an outpatient detox program. After that he had seemed to be himself again—for a while.

He said he did not know what had happened to cause his nervous disorientation. He was shivering, so I held him close and then I saw it—a dark bruise in the hollow of his right elbow.

"Robin, what did you do?" I cried, panicked.

He folded up his arm and would not let me pry it open. I was not wearing my glasses. Perhaps I imagined it?

Suddenly, Robin was so reassuring. He seemed to be himself again, relaxed and in control. Later he would tell me that he had "tried to inject something, Mom, but I couldn't do it."

I was stupid and desperate enough to believe that explanation. In the past several months when I had tried to confront Robin about drug use, he had looked me in the eye and said, "You don't have to worry about me, Mom".

But I had worried about Robin. The year after Arthur died, Robin moved into a house with a friend for a year, and when I saw him, his behavior concerned me. I knew that he was really troubled by his father's death but unlike his sister, refused to see anyone who might talk to him about his grief. He was the one who had been with Arthur that day in 2002, when Becky and I were somewhere over the Pacific returning from a curtailed visit to my family in the UK, and Arthur was succumbing to the effects of a devastating stroke. I often recall that day as we waited for Robin in the frosty midnight air outside the airport, too tired to wonder much why Robin was driving to meet us instead of Arthur. After he had stowed our luggage, we got in the car and he told us what had happened. Many times I will think with painful regret of the suffering that day of the two men in my life who were most important to me.

Arthur had been paralyzed from the neck down, mute and very ill with only eye blinks for communication, and he remained that way for the twelve days until he died. Every evening Robin would come from school or work and sit by Arthur's hospital bed, holding his hand. He was very troubled by Arthur's death. He had cared for his father in his distress, while I, the doctor was unavailable. During phone calls from the UK I had sensed something odd about Arthur's doctor-given diagnosis of "migraine" and changed my flight plans, but none of us had an inkling of the impending stroke until the day it happened. I felt very bad about that, but I saw that Robin felt guilt too, for not being able to get his father the right kind of help. But he did all that he could—and so much more. Nevertheless he often seemed to worry about it and even looked depressed at times.

The day I saw that bruise— imagined or not—I asked Robin to join me for a session with the addiction/intervention counselor I had been consulting, and he agreed. I was so encouraged and optimistic about having help for him and for myself. Unfortunately, the session did not go well and Robin seemed nervous and suspicious of the counselor. He did say, however, that he would come back for another visit in a week.

Our short conversation in the car that May morning was the only one we had after that visit. Robin had asked to talk to me a few days earlier, but when I was available, he was with friends and did not want to talk. He did come to my bedroom one night, to chat at 2 am, but I was too sleepy. Now I wish that I had sat up and had that chat.

Later on that Monday, I drove slowly home into our hilly neighborhood, above the blue lake and snowy mountains to the east. The trees were lush and green and the rhododendrons and azaleas were wild with color. I saw a neighbor walking her dog, laughing with a friend. I realized that it had been two years since her daughter had died in a car accident.

"You can survive the death of a child," I thought. Perhaps that thought was a premonition.

At home, I heard Robin's phone ring several times and realized that I had not heard his voice in answer. I ran downstairs and knocked on his bedroom door.

"Hey, Robin, are you awake?"

Silence.

I knocked more loudly as his door was usually locked.

Again—silence.

Now concerned I climbed the stairs and walked outside to call through his bedroom window. I hoped he would be sleeping deeply. He had done this once before.

The air was still warm and the window was open. I looked in.

No! Robin! He was on the floor by his bed and his upper body had fallen over and was trapped between the bed and night-stand. I leapt through the window. Later I would see the huge bruise on my thigh and Becky would find my shuffled off shoes by the wall below the window. I wept and hugged his cool stiffening body and saw the white shoelace around his right arm. I did not know what to do. I looked for a phone and tripped over something— his long legs on the floor.

And then there were paramedics, friends, Becky, the police. I was in shock. I would be in shock for months. It was a strange numbness that allowed me to function, to have a memorial, to be with friends, and especially with Robin's friends who were now so important to me— a living connection with my son. I held onto Becky but she was as shocked as I was. Together over the years we would support each other and to a therapist's question:" How have you and your mother dealt with your brother's death?" she would say, "I would not have survived without my mother and she would not have survived without me."

It is now almost five years since Robin died. After he died, I did not want to think a day ahead. The advent of the New Year—2007—was so hard. I did not want to leave 2006, the last year I had seen and held him. I have a photo of Robin beside my bed. It's the last thing I see before I fall asleep and the first after I open my eyes in the morning. It was taken at my birthday dinner in April 2006, just three days before his 24th birthday. In the photo he is half-smiling, his gray-blue eyes looking directly at the camera, and his blond hair framing his face in curls. I had not seen his curly hair since he was a teenager and started to shave his beautiful locks. There is a light growth of reddish, blond hair on his upper lip and chin. I had wondered if the hair growth was intentional or if it reflected the inertia that seemed to overtake him in those last few months.

There are photos of Robin everywhere in the house and a collage lovingly assembled by one of his artistic friends. I still weep over pictures but increasingly I look at some and remember what an energetic and funny little boy he was, and I laugh aloud.

Why was I so blind? Was I stupid? How could I not have seen that he was seriously addicted to OxyContin®? Was it a form of denial or recognition that I had so little influence over his life any longer? I hoped I could fix or heal Robin. My whole professional life has been about helping heal children and providing comfort. I tried so much to alter the course of that fatal trajectory and I failed. There is so much I will never know, but that has not stopped me from trying to understand, from wrestling with the awful guilt of all that I missed, and the everlasting regret that I could not save my son.

We think we can control the lives of our children. We follow a plan and expect that the results will be as we predict and sometimes, they are. We think that our success is all because of our hard work and choices, but is it? The older I get, the more I believe that we are where we are and who we are because of our genes, our environment and sheer luck or grace. We think we can keep our children safe. We give them our values and expect them to be good citizens. We imagine that we can immunize them against social ills by teaching them about drugs and sex and misadventure and by keeping them busy. We warn them, restrict them, hover over them, and are astonished when their independent natures foil our plans and outwit us.

I remember an evening in 2004 when Robin and I were talking:

"Mom, you did not know that I had a real problem with meth—but I stopped using it."

"You stopped on your own—isn't it terribly addictive?"

Was that why he'd lost his voice occasionally? Was that why he liked to eat so many icy popsicles? Should I have known that methamphetamine users burn their throats? I'd been horrified but also relieved. He had stopped himself. Perhaps he would escape the addictions that had troubled his father and an uncle, both of whom had sobered up as mature adults. And so when I had a concern about OxyContin, I thought that he would be able to deal with that, too.

There is so much I will never know and so much to imagine. I have tortured myself with guilt about missed opportunities, about my denial, and my inability to get help. I wonder how I, a flawed human being, influenced our darling son, and how our marriage and genes could have contributed to his addiction.

Even today, I am not sure what I would have done differently, but the "what if's" keep me humble—if not abjectly guilty any more. Surviving this awful experience helps me understand the imperfect nature of life and the struggles of others. I work for a foundation that helps addicted young people and their families and supports education and research into the causes of addiction. And, it has become a passion of mine to use my knowledge to help others and especially to educate other doctors about the dangers of overprescribing narcotic drugs. Many now recognize that OxyContin is synthetic heroin. Until Robin died I had no awareness of the widespread availability of OxyContin and other potent opiates. I did not recognize the particular attraction of OxyContin—oxycodone packaged for a timed release, and therefore a very large pure dose of potent opiate in a small innocent-looking pill.

I met other bereaved family members online and locally, and began to grasp the extent of the devastation caused by the unwitting prescribing of these drugs, mostly unused and left in medicine cupboards. In 1996, doctors were told that pain was not being treated properly and that we must start to do so, by asking all our patients about the degree of their pain and then medicating it. The pendulum swung so far from the concerns we had that everyone who was given an opiate would become an addict, to the belief that if the medication was used only for pain, that addiction would be a rare phenomenon. As a consequence, opiates were prescribed in large amounts for self-limited and acute pain. I read widely about the origins of the epidemic of death and addiction and was startled to read of the escalating deaths by overdose.

And so, I found a purpose and a way to honor Robin's life and experience. I began to see that my voice as a doctor and a bereaved parent might give people pause. It was in July 2010 that I found the motivation to speak out more. I heard about a meeting of the FDA in Washington DC where an expert committee would convene to advise the FDA about strategies to educate doctors about risks associated with opiate use and widespread prescribing. With a day to go before the deadline I applied and wrote about my knowledge of physician practice and my personal experience, asking to attend—and was thrilled when I was given a slot to speak. I managed to get a few days off work and started to create my presentation. All speakers would have three minutes at the podium. I worked harder and with more passion on my words and PowerPoint slides than I ever had on an academic presentation, rehearsing and timing myself until I was satisfied that I could say all that was necessary in the allotted three minutes.

I was nervous but filled with the strength of my convictions that July day, and when my name was called to speak before the many experts in that room, I spoke about Robin's death, the deaths of some of his friends and acquaintances, the struggles with addiction in people I knew and the many struggling and dying nationwide—all because of prescription drugs. I told them that accidental deaths from prescription drug overdose had exceeded death from car accidents in many of our states. I said that I was not against treatment of pain but that I believed that we should use the many other options for treatment and not medication alone, recognizing that the pressure on doctors to see more patients in a given time—and the desire in our culture for quick relief—made it difficult for practitioners to resist prescribing the quick solution of an opiate drug. I ended with a quote from Robin, to which I wish I had paid more attention or asked more questions:

"Mom, you have to see—doctors are the biggest drug pushers in the country."

Robin is forever my cherished 24-year-old son who died too soon. But he is so much more than that. He brought me great joy. He was loved by his father and his sister, and his many friends. He was smart, handsome, adventurous and protective of others. Sometimes, I feel his presence and sense that he is encouraging me to tell others what I now know, so that perhaps one life will be saved.

The Ambulance and then the RV

By Andrea Margaret Franzen

IN THE GRAND SCHEME OF THE WORLD, I had very few things to complain about growing up. But like most kids, I was certain I'd arrived on this earth by way of the weirdest parents of all time.

After growing up in the city, getting married and buying a house in Minneapolis, my parents decided one day to buy a forty-acre farm and become farmers. Having never farmed, this proved to be a challenge. And for them, a shining example of what would become a recurring theme in their lives, and as a result, my life: adventure (for them) mixed with total chaos (for everyone involved). These two charming features proved time and time again to be grounds for wishing long and hard that I could trade in my parents for a new pair. It's taken me nearly thirty-two years to realize I actually adore those qualities, and that my parents, despite having never done anything in what would be considered a normal way, are wonderfully unique and loveable in their own little way. And really, it is by way of adventure and total chaos I can only *hope* I am able to live my life.

When I was in the fifth grade I joined the famed Girl Scouts, but learned quickly that success in terms of Girl Scout cookie sales was limited to those whose dad or mom worked in an office and displayed the sign-up sheet prominently spawning lucrative orders. Instead, my father generated a modest income raising yearly rotating crops of corn, soybeans and alfalfa, alongside pigs, cattle and chickens that we mostly raised and then consumed, which included beheading the chickens ourselves. I can remember my father giving the bird a big whack and it then was our responsibility as children to chase the running headless animal and catch it. He supplemented farming by working as a small-engine mechanic driving around a truck full of tools fixing peoples' broken lawn mowers, chainsaws and snow blowers. His angle: He was like a delivery guy in that his service came to you, and he fixed things in the driveways and garages of his customers' homes. *Voila*, a traveling mechanic.

My mother, a self-proclaimed "artist and free spirit," started her career working for Northwest Airlines but soon saw the parenting benefits of self-employment. First, she started Creative Paper and Paint, generating business by word of mouth painting and wallpapering sometimes every single room in a client's home – a profession that left the interiors of our vehicles covered in various forms of spilled paint. There was never an obvious place to actually *sit* because her cars were filled to the ceiling with paint trays, rollers, garbage, soda cans, papers, and endless cigarette butts. Several years later my mother started a second business doing custom framing, working out of a self-made studio in one of our barns. She was incredibly talented but lacked discipline, resulting in orders taking months or even several years to fulfill. Basically, the two of them used any means, and the bulk of their talents, to provide for our family.

If I had to describe the space for which my childhood occupied, the image I would conjure would include heaps and heaps of Stuff. There has never been a phase throughout the course of their lives where my parents lived with an abundance of money, and as a team they never underestimated the power of value. Value in this case meaning: Save everything. Any item could be fixed or enhanced and sold for profit. Something that lacked any sort of immediate identifiable value was still a viable candidate for later value.

Thinking of the profit of things became a way of life and gave rise to a process I like to call: Wheelin' and Dealin'. My Pops was *always* Wheelin' and Dealin' and alas, we needed places to house all the value potential. Pantry shelves were stuffed with last year's after-Christmas door-buster deals. The basement had at least nineteen televisions, none of which actually worked – yet. They filled up closets and spilled out into the surrounding farm structures; a lawnmower graveyard occupied a large poll barn, and my dad could be found scouring the bodies for parts to sell off one-by-one for profit. The Stuff was overwhelming and the prospect of having a sleepover on a whim was nonexistent as we needed at least a month of preparation for any chance at a socially acceptable house.

My parents weren't exactly the type-A parents when managing the Stuff either. For years I longed for the parents who organized garage sales for all their unused and unwanted things, and applied color-coordinated, round stickers neatly indicating prices. A golden opportunity to offload unwanted possessions onto others, making room for space and sanity, all for the sake of shiny profit. My parents weren't the kind who hosted garage sales though, and in fact, my parents weren't like anyone else's parents.

Our family cars, which were also acquired through the aforementioned Wheelin' and Dealin' process, included a trip to an auction where damaged, post-accident vehicles sold for cheap. My father and his skilled worker pals would buy and fix up the cars themselves, except they were usually only fixed to about 70% completion and therefore a ride in one of our cars was never without its quirks. Maybe it was a door that could only be opened a couple of inches leaving you to slither inside, an exterior toggle switch that activated the air conditioning, or *maybe,* it was a used ambulance with no actual seats in the back. Yep.

To be a traveling mechanic, my father needed a very large van and when the normal one broke down around the same time he started going to the car auctions, he discovered that an old ambulance works just as good as any van. And with the slap of a Suburban Small Engine logo on the side, Pops was back in business. Ninety percent of the time my ambulance-driving-dad-embarrassment was tucked away in our driveway. But occasionally, when Mom was busy or her paint car wasn't working properly, I'd see the ambulance round the corner into the school parking lot to pick me up from volleyball practice.

"Is your dad driving an *ambulance*?" someone would always ask as we all milled around outside the double-doors.

"Um, *nooo.* No that's his work truck. See the logo on the side?" I'd say like it was unequivocal.

Then I'd climb up into the front seat and admonish him on the way home with a healthy dose of the silent treatment.

I know it seems a bit obvious that a child eventually experiences a moment of realized acceptance and love for their parents. I guess I just wasn't expecting mine, and I could have never predicted how it would unfold.

Five years ago I moved to Seattle. Slowly, the distance created a certain appreciation that didn't exist in the world where we were accessible to each other in a twenty minute drive. Then, I went home last Christmas and I sat shotgun to my dad in his enormous, rusty plow truck as he cleared away what seemed like endless amounts of snow from the driveway. I watched him work and smiled, stealing a few rare and sweet father-daughter moments alone. As the monster plow shoved colossal mouthfuls of Minnesota snow my dad struck up an unorthodox conversation.

"You know, I'm not going to be around much longer. And someone's gonna have to help your mother take care of things."

Insert awkward pause. Followed by sudden feelings of panic.

"Umm, Dad, *why* would you *say* something like that?" I said, unable to articulate what I really wanted to say as it wasn't typical for my family to actually *talk* about a lot of emotional things.

"Well, I'm just sayin'. There are a lot of things around here that she's going to need help with."

"Oh." My mind raced. And as the silence ticked by in the truck I knew the conversation was over. That my father didn't want to talk about it, and in his own way he had said what he needed to say, and that was it.

Later, I finally found my mother alone in the kitchen, "So, is Dad sick or something?" I practically threw the words at her. "Because...he was talking about how he's not going to be around much longer and stuff, when we were in the plow truck. Is there something going on? That you haven't told us?"

"Naaa, your father's just being all morbid." She replied with a heavy sigh as if describing a finicky neighbor's mood. "He's been to the doctor and his counts are all good. I think he's just a little down, ya know? Feeling old."

I felt better knowing my mother was all but irritated, but still, I couldn't shake the vision my Pops had planted: the inevitability of their demise. He was only sixty-two, and in relatively good health so I suppose until now I'd managed to avoid thinking about my parents in such a way. That split second of uncertainty in the plow truck however had flashed a whole picture of existence without him.

Later in the spring, an unexpected meeting would exponentially change everything. My lovely and dear Portland friends, Lindsay and Matthew, announced they were planning a six-month road trip across America in an Airstream trailer. When they called with the news, they also had a favor. The Airstream trailer search had been an arduous one, but a viable candidate happened to be sitting on a farm in Minnesota. Would it be possible for my parents to give it a look over and maybe decide if the trailer was legit and the seller wasn't crazy?

My parents had never met Lindsay and Matthew, but the trailer was not far from their house and they were happy to help. My mother gave the inside her complete inspection and my dad crawled underneath to look for anything glaringly wrong mechanically. Eventually, they gave the trailer a thumbs up, but not without some classic feedback from frugal Pops, "Pretty spendy for a tin can." Sold!

The Airstream pick-up included a stop at my parents' farm to meet them and say thank you. Several Hamm's beers washed down stories and laughter as the four of them got to know each other and eventually my friends, at my parents' insistence, spent their first night in their Airstream parked in my parents' driveway. The following morning they awoke to an elaborate slideshow my Pops excitedly put together, dug up from a dusty box containing images of traveling adventures in Africa, Asia and Europe when my parents were in their twenties and my mom worked for the airlines.

Lindsay and Matthew would later describe their experience on the farm as being profound and inspirational. My parents' generosities, as well as their history of travel and adventure, and their devoted forty-year marriage were things they hoped to carry out in their own lives. "You come from some pretty amazing roots, girl." Lindsay chirped into the phone from the road. "Your parents are pretty incredible people and they definitely impacted us. Matthew and I can't stop talking about them."

Listening to my friends describe at length their admiration for my parents gave me an objective view of them as people, combined with the collective assemblage of both seeing their eventual departure, and the distance and space to reflect in Seattle, set free a chain reaction of gratitude and appreciation for my parents and their eccentricities. In a relatively short time it was as if they had morphed into different people, different parents, when in reality they were the same and I had changed. My parents are definitely unique. And I guess their unique-ness was a badge I was too afraid to try on in school and in my early twenties, but one I was finally ready to display proudly.

To my surprise and delight, that summer my parents decided to plan a five-week road trip scheduled to depart after Labor Day. Like any normal family would, my dad 'Wheeled and Dealed' an RV, sight unseen, through an online auction.

He called with the news, "Well, I bought an RV." I could hear the smile on his face. "It's out in Eugene, Oregon, by you. She was a good deal and I figger if we get there and she's not great, we can just put'er back up on the auction block and drive a rental back home."

Here we go. *Sure!* Sounds perfectly normal. And at least some things never change. But I sure was proud of them. Their souls had been stirred resulting in the realization that they needed to grab life by the reigns and continue living the tenets of adventure and total chaos with never-ending flair. They began planning their trip and it seemed like every time we spoke on the phone they introduced an incremental element of the journey, each more informed than the last, right up until the day they boarded a plane for the west coast.

When my parents landed in Portland, ironically but also appropri-ately, it was Lindsay and Matthew who took them to meet their new online-purchased RV, but when they flung open the door and peered inside, it was only an empty box. No big and squishy Grandpa chair behind the wheel, or one for his trusty co-pilot. No couch. The origi-nal table had been ripped from the wall, as well as the stove, refrigera-tor, and all of the components that could make up a sink. Sigh.

I was heavy just thinking of my parents in Oregon. I wanted their trip to be lasting and remarkable. I made the assumption the RV would go back on the auction block and the trip would commence – less fun, but just fine – behind the wheel of an Economy Plus. Alas, it did not. How could I have hastily assumed such a thing? Instead, my parents started scoping out Craigslist as well as a local RV World and Home Depot.

"No way, we're gonna fix it up!" Pops called en route to some good deal he'd found on a stove. He passed the phone to my mother.

"*Andrea*, this is just *so* exciting! Do you know that I've *actually* learned something new about your father after forty years of mar-riage?"

"What's that, Mama?" I asked, skeptical of their plight but delighted and relieved to soak in their energy.

"Well, I learned that I like your father a whole lot better when he has a project." And she started laughing hysterically into the phone. I laughed too.

"You should see your father. He's been talking to all his buddies back home and they've all started shopping for their own RVs. They want to travel with us."

I was smiling. A small tear rolled down my cheek as I listened to her descriptions of their plans to fix up the RV and continue the journey, and knowing that if I spoke my voice would surely crack. They were exhilarated and somewhere in this process my dad had started to engage with life again. He realized the depth of what is possible in his life still and if it meant installing a new stove from Craigslist to do it, just like driving around an ambulance, I guess it was all just part of the journey. For him, I had finally realized, these experiences that seemed so strange are what made it all that much more fun and exciting.

Within a week my parents had their RV to well over the standard 70% completion. They had installed club seats in the front, a new sofa, a bed in the back, a sink and microwave, and also that deal of a stove. The missing refrigerator was all but solved by the use a trusty cooler with ice. I thought about the whimsy with which my parents have always lived their lives and I actually felt a pang of jealousy. More than finally seeing my parents as a wonderful part of my life, I now saw them as inspiration—motivation even—for doing the things I want to do in my life and not worrying about doing them in the ways the world around us might expect. Why is it that I spend so much time making sure things are planned and perfect and acceptable?

I thought about a quote I'd once read by Deepak Chopra saying, "The physical world, including our bodies, is a response of the observer. We create our bodies as we create the experience of our world." The fact is, life is really so much our own perception of things. My father had been sure his life was nearly over and now he was sitting behind the wheel of a new adventure and he definitely didn't know how it was going to turn out. And just like him, we can make our lives and our experiences whatever we want them to be.

My parents eventually joined forces with Lindsay and Matthew and they parked their respective wheeled homes next to each other in a small RV park nestled on the shores of the Columbia River, just outside of Portland. Being three hours away in Seattle, my fiancé and I drove down to participate in their great adventure for a few days. Driving along the windy two-lane road flanked by fields and farms, we eventually pulled into the park, slowing to allow several dozen chickens the opportunity to get out of the way. Never could I have predicted the swelling in my heart when we found my parents stretched out in camp chairs on the beach, with *my* friends, on the west coast, in the crazy RV they bought online.

Life is short. Live an adventure. Or just get an RV.

Fashion Statement

By Jeanne Verville

I WAS IN DESPERATE NEED OF A NEW WARDROBE. I was starting a job as Assistant Counsel for Washington's largest privately held corporation. A lawyer of just two years, I had only two suits: a grey and a navy blue. The rest of my wardrobe was mix and match from the sales rack. Though I always looked presentable, I was insecure about how I appeared to others and didn't know the rules of dressing professionally in the big city.

Actually, I was insecure about everything. I had lived in Kansas for sixteen years, starring as traditional wife and mother, and then, in my early forties, I found myself as the oldest kid in my law school class after an acrimonious divorce. I'd left a man who—despite my Phi Beta Kappa key—mocked my intelligence, and I was still amazed I had graduated from law school and found the nerve to pack up and move to Seattle.

At the time, 1987, most female attorneys tried to fit into the male-dominated career of law by downplaying their femininity, so I was in search of well dressed role models who were both powerful and attractive. At a legal seminar, I was fascinated by one speaker in particular. She wore a red double-breasted jacket, a heavy gold necklace that edged her white jewel-neck blouse, a black pencil skirt, off-black hose and a pair of expensive looking black heels. Her hair was short and well-cut. She wore red, red lipstick and makeup that accentuated her dark eyes. *Wow*, I thought, *that's how I want to look! She looks commanding!* She spoke with authority, confident but relaxed enough to throw in some funny asides. Having gone to law school at the age of forty-one to change my life, I felt like a late comer, but I wanted to look and act like that woman.

I knew it would take years to become confident in the practice of law, but in the meantime I could start working on my fashion statement. I knew, but didn't quite believe, that I already had a certain presence because of my maturity and the fact that others saw me as "pretty." If I dressed well, maybe people wouldn't know what a newbie I really was.

With my new role model in mind, I set out to improve my wardrobe. As I had learned from my Depression era mother, I headed for the sale racks at Nordstrom's. I combed through many suits in flat weaves and drab colors, feeling discouraged. Then, there it was -- a raspberry raw silk suit in size ten. It wasn't red, but it was beautiful. The sales woman told me it was a perfect color for me. "According to *Color Me Beautiful,*" she said, "you are a winter."

"What does that mean?" I asked.

"Oh, you *must* get your colors done. But, with your dark hair and eyes and pink and white complexion, I'm sure you're a winter."

My ears perked up. "How do I get my "colors" done?" I asked. I wondered about some of my past failed purchases, mostly in shades of orange and tan, anathema to a "winter" I later learned.

"Oh, just make an appointment with one of our personal stylists. She'll help you."

A couple of weeks after I started my new job, I flew in a private jet down to Redding, California with the company president to tour a pulp and paper mill there. *Wow*, I thought. *This is moving up!* I proudly wore my new raspberry suit.

It was August, and we arrived in 102 degree heat that shimmered on the tarmac. Inside the pulp and paper mill, which covered several acres, steam hissed from huge paper dryers, raising the temperature easily to 125 degrees. In my patent leather heels, I practically had to run to keep up as the president, a former Marine, casually pointed out the basics of paper making as we raced past enormous machines, up several flights of concrete stairs and over wire-mesh catwalks. I jumped across puddles and large hoses, dodging forklifts. The workers, mostly men wearing jeans and sweat-stained t-shirts, looked up from their jobs as I passed by, probably looking like a raspberry bird of paradise in the old, grey industrial setting. Why hadn't anyone warned me to dress down for the mill tour?

The next spring, a neighbor invited me to a party at a big house on Lake Washington. Again, I wore my raspberry suit, which my mother, on a recent visit from the Southwest, had declared "stunning."

"Ohhh," my new friend cooed when I came in the door, her eyebrows arched and her eyes flaring like a racehorse's. "You look so... so...well, so *bright!*"

I blushed and fought the sting of tears. Looking around, I noted the many shades of black, grey, and earth tones—sophisticated Seattle's color palette. I left early.

I was desperate to learn the rules. After struggling through law school, as a single parent, I wanted my new career to work for me. And, not wishing to remain forever single, I also wanted to fit into Seattle's fashionable social scene, where I hoped I'd find my Mr. Right.

Not long after this, I went to a Washington Women Lawyers' meeting, held in a sleek law firm conference room. Whenever I went to a legal meeting or event, I made it a point to come away with at least one date for coffee or lunch. I knew very few people in Seattle and wanted to build a network. One woman, Pat, whom I'd met at other meetings, was especially friendly to me when she heard that I'd gone back to law school after I had children, as she herself had done. When I heard Pat's story of rising to partner in a prestigious firm while raising a family, I felt great admiration. We agreed to meet for lunch.

We met at Palomino's, a popular restaurant in her office tower that served "modern" Italian food. Pat was wearing a grey suit with a pearl necklace and an expensive looking watch. She looked authoritative yet not forbidding. I had on my navy suit, which was developing shiny elbows, and a pale yellow oxford and one of my boxy little ties. After the failure of my raspberry suit, I hadn't had the confidence to get out there and shop again and I felt slightly shabby in this glittering new restaurant, surrounded by established looking professionals. I wasn't used to fancy restaurants with brass railings and hand-blown glass chandeliers, and I still hadn't accepted that I, now a professional, belonged here.

Halfway through the meal, over the clang of the kitchen and buzz of the crowded room, Pat said, "Jeanne, do you have a plan for your wardrobe?"

"Well, uh, no, I mean, what do you mean?" I mumbled, looking down. I knew that to appear to be on top of things, it was important to have a plan, so I quickly changed my tack. "I have a plan to get a better wardrobe but I'm afraid of making mistakes, which I can't afford."

"I've noticed that you seem to wear the same things over and over. I thought you might be in the initial stages of building a wardrobe. May I give you some suggestions?"

"That would be great," I said quietly, feeling both ashamed of my limited wardrobe, and grateful that maybe I'd found a friend.

"First," she said, "you need to think of spending money on clothes as making an investment in yourself. It isn't so hard to spend money if you think of the cost per wearing."

"I'm sorry. I don't know what you mean?" I said, and took a sip of water.

"If you buy a good suit for $250 and wear it fifty times, that's five dollars a wearing. Is it worth five dollars to look terrific in the boardroom and when trying to impress your clients and other lawyers? *Looking* successful helps you feel confident and makes it easier to *become* a successful."

I felt excited but a little daunted. The truth was that as much as I wanted to build a wardrobe and look the part, the thought of how much that would cost was, frankly, a bit scary. A female lawyer on the new show *LA Law,* which I watched religiously, mentioned in one episode that she spent $3,000 a year on clothes: $3,000! Could I afford that? My two girls were teenagers and I didn't want to shortchange their needs. How could I justify spending my limited income on *myself?*

Pat must have sensed my thoughts. She leaned forward and looked me straight in the eyes. "What you wear expresses who you are and affects how other people react to you. It really *can* affect your future." She sounded like a lawyer making her case to the jury.

I knew that was true, sort of. I learned as a teenager in the conformist 1950s, that it was important to dress like a lady (modestly) and to dress as well as possible (to reflect social status). It was important to buy good quality, wear good (and polished) shoes and have a good haircut. My mother had prepared me well to become a successful wife and mother. I sensed that Pat was taking up where Mother left off.

"It's important that your clothes have authority," Pat continued. "Have you read *The Woman's Dress for Success Book*?"

"No," I answered, again looking down. *Am I a bumpkin?* I wondered for a second. I knew I wasn't. My mother had always been stylish. I had gone to a finishing school in Chicago, worked in New York City and Denver and had always been complimented on my appearance. No, I was just afraid. I was so insecure that deep down I felt it would be deceptive to *appear* more successful than I really was.

Pat continued on. "I suggest you read it and make an appointment with a personal stylist at Nordstrom's. She'll analyze your figure and make recommendations. She'll know the stock in the entire store and even help you with accessories and jewelry. If you want to climb the ladder of success, you must take yourself seriously or others won't."

I was sold. I bought the book *and* went to the stylist, who confirmed that I was indeed a "winter." She told me I needed petites on top and regulars on the bottom and quickly put together two new outfits for me. She even picked out some large "corporate" gold earrings and an expensive silk scarf I would never even have looked at to teach me how to tie an outfit together.

"There," she said, as I stared into the three panel mirror. "You look like an established attorney." It was true. I did! My heart turned summersaults.

Over the next months I bought two more suits—class B suits—nice, but not Dana Buchman or Ellen Tracy. They still seemed *way* too expensive. But I was making progress. I bought only natural fabrics (wool, cotton, silk) and stuck to muted colors, which I learned conferred authority. My Nordy's angel kept refining my look. She *made* me buy a pair of black, sling-back pumps, instructing me to avoid open toes. They smelled so good—so genuinely leather—and, with my mother's shapely ankles, I felt very sophisticated in them.

One day my stylist, tilting her head to one side, said, "Jeanne, I think you should have one of our cosmetics experts advise you on makeup. I think you're wearing the wrong color lipstick and blusher. And I strongly suggest you stop wearing those L'eggs hose—the colors and texture aren't refined enough." I dutifully followed orders. Of course, fine hosiery cost three times my grocery store L'eggs. But I was slowly letting go of my worn out belief that it was selfish to spend money on myself.

The makeup "specialist," whose skin was flawless, talked me into a three-step skin treatment adding up to $120. "Buy only red-blue shades of lipstick and blusher," she said. "Avoid earthy colors. Also, avoid black eyeliner. It's too harsh for your age."

The cost of my fashion statement was now $1,500 per year! I was shocked. But I wanted to be successful, so I stuck with my plan.

The company I worked for was doing very well and was generous in sending me to legal seminars to learn new areas of the law. Usually, the seminars were in Seattle, sometimes in Portland. One fall, my boss sent me to New York City. I guiltily skipped two sessions on the last day and took the subway to the lower east side and Orchard Street's small, unadorned discount stores.

In the very first shop, which resembled a trailer home inside, I ended up buying two Christian Dior suits at half price. One was beautiful jade green wool, with a mid-calf skirt and a longish jacket that boasted big shoulder pads. The sales woman told me that shoulder pads helped women project power. I questioned the green as possibly too "bright" but decided it was appropriately subtle. The other suit was medium taupe wool, with a pleated skirt and lapelled jacket. *I can wear this around color phobics*, I thought. I left the shop feeling so excited the hairs on the back of my neck tingled.

In the second shop I bought a peachy-pink silk blouse with attached tie for the taupe suit and a green and black speckled silk scarf for the green.

I felt special. *Christian Dior*. My wardrobe had taken a big bump up in status. And I didn't guilty at the $250 per I spent. *It's an investment*, I told myself.

A week later, I wore the taupe suit on a plane to Scottsdale for a legal meeting. The handsome man sitting next to me told me I looked "lovely" and asked if I had plans for dinner that night. My investments were paying dividends. And I thought that maybe I should start exploring silky, lacy undergarments.

The next month, on a business trip to San Francisco, I clicked through the Financial District in my black sling-backs, enjoying the delicious swish of expensive green wool on my calves. *I felt pretty... oh so pretty...* I felt confident as I entered the office tower. I wasn't an expert on the natural gas contracts I would be discussing with the senior lawyer in this prestigious law firm, but didn't worry because I always seemed to know enough. I was learning to trust that my hard work was paying off.

One day, while wearing my taupe Christian Dior, my boss told me I had developed "presence" and that the company executives thought well of me. Shortly after, I was promoted. And, after giving a speech at a seminar, a well-known tall, dark and handsome lawyer asked me for a date. Not long after, I was entrusted with organizing lunches for the bar association I belonged to and felt completely comfortable introducing luminaries from Washington D.C. and New York. Soon, Washington Women Lawyers asked me if I would consider running for president of the county chapter, and then I was asked to sit on the State Gender and Justice Commission. ·

After ten years, I had a closet full of good clothes, some bought on sale, some not, most of reasonable cost. I had styles and fabrics that flattered my figure and coloring. Because of that, my wardrobe was flexible and I could mix and match with confidence. I followed my own artistic nature by accessorizing with unusual scarves and jewelry, so my look had some individuality. I didn't agonize about what to wear each day. I just reached into the closet and put something on, confident my attire said what I wanted it to say.

One day I gave a presentation to a group of prominent general counsels. I was a little nervous, but took a deep breath and reminded myself that I always seemed to land on my feet. I wore my Nancy Reagan red jacket with a black pencil skirt, black pumps and notice-ably good earrings. I spoke from my own knowledge on a complex subject with few notes and interjected bits of humor without effort. Every face was attentive. My boss, with a big smile on his face, told me that several of the attendees told him it was the best speech they'd heard in years.

I'd worked hard, learned to wear the right uniform while retaining my own personality, and had become a successful role model for younger female attorneys. And *that* was a very satisfying feeling.

A Sign on the Door

Abigail Carter

WE DROVE DOWN THE BUMPY GRAVEL DRIVEWAY towards a red barn
with white trim, surrounded by lush green gardens, looking much like
a barn a child might draw. The proprietor was not there. She had told
me ahead of time she had taken the weekend off to go "shrimping."

"It's the only weekend of the year I can do this. Just come into the
barn and go right up to the top to the 'Loft.' The door will be open."

We were on Vashon Island for the weekend to celebrate Mother's
Day and my friend Deirdre's mother's birthday. Deirdre's small cabin
wouldn't fit both her family and mine, so I had rented a room in the
loft of this barn for my two kids and I. It turned out this was a famous
barn. It was once owned by Betty MacDonald, the 1940s author of
the popular, comedic memoir, *The Egg and I,* and the *Miss Piggle Wig-
gle* series of children's books.

Mother's Day was still a difficult day for me, despite the six years
that had passed since my husband Arron died suddenly. Though the
misshapen pancakes our kids made always made me laugh and I mar-
veled at the increasing sophistication of my annual breakfast in bed
with additions such as snow-dustings of powdered sugar and orange
slices arranged artfully around the outside rim of the plate – I could
never help noticing what was missing. I remembered his misshapen
pancakes (meant to be Minnie Mouse), brought up on a tray jiggling
in our daughter's five-year old grip. Arron, in his ratty blue terry cloth
bathrobe bent with hands under the tray, ready to catch it if it fell.
Our son followed, a bottle in his mouth as he clutched his ear. Moth-

er's Day always ended the moment I finished the pancakes and Arron took the tray, saying "are you gonna stay in bed all day?"

After he died, he seemed to find ways of making his presence known —lights or CD players turned on inexplicably, in the lingering aroma of a wood burning fireplace in our bedroom, timely, healing books that found their way into my hands at just the right moment, a hawk or a butterfly flying by as I thought of him. Each sign seemed to carry a significant message as if he were trying to guide me through a life without him.

In recent years, the signs had been waning from my life, in a way that made me feel both sad and proud—sad that he was becoming a less tangible presence in my life and proud that perhaps I didn't need his signs anymore, that I was stronger now and capable of conducting my life without his ghostly presence.

As I approached the barn with Deirdre and our kids behind me, I noticed a piece of paper tacked to the door that read "Arron Place" in big loopy writing. It had a hand-drawn arrow pointing to the left, presumably to the "cottage" where I had been told an "Aaron" would be staying that same weekend. Reading the name, with its unique double 'r' spelling didn't seem unusual. In fact, I thought the directions were meant for me, unconsciously registering Arron's name as my own.

"That is just too weird!" Deirdre said. "Why is Arron's name on here? Do they know about Arron?"

Seeing Arron's name made me feel tingly, slightly weak. "No." I said, momentarily confused. "I think the sign is for another person who is staying in the other room. Weird that his name is Arron with two R's though."

"Yeah," Deirdre said. "Really weird."

I hesitated at the door, not sure if I should follow the arrow or proceed through the slightly open barn door.

"I guess we just go in," I said, and opened the door wider. Deirdre, her daughter Rosemary, my daughter Olivia and son Carter entered a dark cavernous space with cement floors. Immediately to our right was a staircase, which we crept up, feeling like intruders. A one-eyed cat appeared, smoothing its body against Olivia's legs, pleased to see people. Another omen? Olivia squealed and bent down to pet the cat. We wandered through the second floor of the barn's almost empty spaces. Sunlight filtered through the dirty windows and illuminated delicate watercolors of flowers pinned to the white washed walls, an easel in the corner, a table strewn with crumpled tubes of colored paints, and an ancient typewriter.

"Cool! Is this a typewriter?" Carter asked when he saw it, pushing his fingers against the keys, watching in fascination as a long, thin, spidery leg tapped a square lettered foot onto the paperless roller. Beside the typewriter, a montage of Betty MacDonald's book covers leaned haphazardly against the wall. On another wall, an old map of Vashon from the 1920s showed not only the names of roads, but also the names of each landowner and the boundaries of their properties. I studied it for a few minutes, fascinated. We found a tiny door at the top of a narrow set of stairs leading to what seemed to be an attic. A wooden sign with the word "Loft" spray-painted in green was our only clue that we were in the right place. The cat followed us up.

The room we entered was dark and mystical, walls hung with antique African drums and framed etchings; tables covered with tall, haphazard stacks of books and magazines; Persian rugs carpeted every surface including the home-made couch created from wide cedar planks and topped with huge kilim pillows. A small, cluttered kitchen built from more cedar was overhung with pots and pans. Open shelves held mismatched dishes and flowery fabric skirted the lower shelving. The back wall of the room was windowed with French doors opening onto a small balcony and overlooked a well-kept perennial garden. A burgundy enameled Vermont Castings woodstove filled one corner, a tidy stack of wood piled beside it. At the other end of the room, stood an over-sized, satin-covered wrought iron bed next to a white vinyl chaise lounge covered in a faux fur-like blanket. Antique, glass-door bookshelves housed worn, leather-bound volumes of Dickens, gardening books and old editions of "English Garden" magazines.

"I've never seen any place like this!" Deirdre exclaimed, plugging in a string of red chili-pepper-shaped lights that hung over the kitchen alcove. "This place is amazing!"

"I wonder if some of these books might have belonged to Betty MacDonald?" I said as I ran my finger along the entire set of faded green, leather-bound Dickens.

"Someone needs to get married and have their wedding here!"

"Yeah, that would be cool. Don't look at me though..." I smiled.

"We *have* to have dinner here tonight!" Deirdre clapped her hands together.

Later that night, after a dinner of take-out ribs and coleslaw from the local grocery store, the kids played Scrabble. Michael, a friend who had arrived late from work, joined them on the floor still dressed in his suit. Jack, Deirdre's husband had left to visit his sister, who also lived on the island, so Deirdre and I settled into the large room and explored books and magazines.

"Look at this!" I said. I handed her a folder full of old postcards and a section of newspaper dated May 15, 1929. Deirdre was immediately taken by line drawings depicting women reposing on their couches, feet resting on long cylindrical cushions with tassels on the ends, something you might see in a Turkish opium den.

"These cushions must have been all the rage back then. Every picture in this home section shows one. They are so cool! Why haven't they come back in fashion? I totally want one!"

Later that night, Deirdre drove Michael's car back to her cabin. Michael chose to crash on one of the Kilim-covered couches. Rosemary and Olivia giggled in the tiny bedroom where they discovered the wall dividing their room from the bathroom didn't extend all the way to the floor and they could crawl under the bed into the bathroom. Carter read an Archie comic book beside me in bed while I read my own book.

In the morning, Mother's Day, the girls made scrambled eggs, refusing to let me help. Carter helped Michael light a fire in the woodstove to offset the cool grey morning. I continued to explore the stacks of books and magazines and came across a book called *Love: Penhaligon's Scented Treasury of Verse and Prose*. It was a tiny hardback volume that fit into its own sleeve. *Love*, I thought sardonically. *Not for me anymore*.

I wanted to see if the volume was indeed scented, so I opened the book and sniffed at it, disappointed by its lack of fragrance. It fell open to a painting that I had seen before – a medieval era image of a flame-haired maiden leaning down from a white horse to kiss her knight in shining armor. It took me a moment to recognize it as the exact same image on the tenth wedding anniversary card that I had given Arron the year before he died. In the top left corner of the page was a poem, something that hadn't been on the card. Reading it, I was as shocked as if it had been written in Arron's own handwriting. His secret message to me from beyond, a secret Mother's Day message turned out to be a Lord Byron poem, "So We'll Go No More A-Roving." My melancholy Mother's Day mood vanished. I showed Michael the book, and explained the significance of the painting.

"That's amazing! But it doesn't surprise me. Stuff like this is always happening to you."

'Yeah, I guess that's sort of true."

"Did you see the author's name on the front of the book?" He held up the cover for me to see.

"Sheila Pickles." A name that could have been coined by Arron himself, having long ago given Olivia the nickname "Picklehorse."

"Ohmygosh! That can *not* be a coincidence!"

A month later the kids and I spent a week on Vashon Island with Deirdre's daughter Rosemary. We stayed in Deirdre's cabin while Carter spent four days at Pirate Camp and Olivia and Rosemary took horseback riding lessons. I crisscrossed the island on the cliché Seattleite's fantasy tour of Vashon Island real estate. I wasn't seriously in the market, but if I found something great, I was willing to consider buying a summer cottage, a cozy one-room cabin perhaps, like Deirdre's tiny hide-away. I found a sweet, brightly painted house on a 48-foot wide lot, where I could barely stand upright in some of the rooms. My kids dubbed it the "doll house" and begged me to buy it. I considered it until the night I had a dream that the kids were all grown up and as teenagers were too tall to stand in the cottage's diminutive kitchen during a party.

I looked at a house that required long trips using a wheelbarrow to cart a weekend's worth of supplies to the front door. I traipsed through the endless, nonsensical rooms of a poorly renovated farmhouse; I stood on a rickety balcony overlooking a beautiful harbor, separated from the house by a busy highway.

On our last night before heading back to the city, I flipped through the Real Estate magazine that the realtor had tucked into a folder now full of the listings of the houses I had seen and landed upon a picture of a stone fireplace and the words "Betty MacDonald's House" jumping off the page. It seemed impossible. I had not seen anything like a stone fireplace in the barn that I had assumed was her house. Was this another sign from Arron? The house cost triple the amount of my "fantasy cabin in the woods" budget.

The next day, I coyly asked J.R., my indulging real estate agent, if it would be possible to see Betty MacDonald's house. I had no intention of buying it because of the price, but I was curious to see it.

"I always thought the barn was Betty MacDonald's house," I said to J.R.

"Oh no. She built the barn after *The Egg and I* was published in order to raise chickens and sell eggs again, you know, to capitalize on the egg thing." J.R. petted her tiny dog, Pixel, a tiny white fluff that I had learned to keep my hands clear of.

"Oh. That makes sense. I couldn't see her living in that barn." J. R. laughed.

"No, that wouldn't be Betty's style, I'm sure."

"I know it's way out of my price range," I said, "but I seem to have an odd connection with Betty."

"It will certainly be an emotional purchase for whoever buys it," J.R. seemed to warn me.

Later that afternoon, on our way out of town, the kids and I followed J.R.'s shiny white pick-up and we found ourselves bumping down a familiar road.

"Mommy, look! There's Betty MacDonald's Farm," Olivia said pointing out the window at the big red barn. "Remember we stayed there?"

"Oh!" I said surprised. "Yes, that's the barn we stayed at." It didn't occur to me that the house would be close to the barn. I followed J.R slowly down the steep, narrow road, trying not to look over the cliff on the passenger side of the road, while the kids let out big whoops of "Ohmygod, don't drive off the road! This is so scary Mama!" At the bottom we parked on a wide plank platform that seemed to cling to the hillside. No house was visible until we began walking down the stone path, shrouded in trees and shrubs. J.R. stood outside the thick wooden door fumbling with the lock box.

We came in through the laundry room and into the kitchen. The aroma of the house immediately brought me back to my grandparent's cottage in Quebec—cedar, dust, long-extinguished fireplace fires, and something sweet, like chocolate chip cookies, so many batches made over the years that the smell was baked into the wood of the kitchen cabinets. The kitchen was dark with its pine cabinetry and radiant terracotta floors, a floor J. R. explained, that was made to Betty's own specifications, though the heat source was no longer functional. The countertops mimicked the floor tiles. I had the disorienting sense that I had stepped back in time to the late 1940s, to a simpler life, and oddly felt as if I was home, or at least back to a place I had once held dear. I barely saw the details of the rest of the house, as the kids raced through each room at lightning speed, quickly discovering the tiny doll-like bedrooms upstairs behind the huge stone fireplace, the focal point of the spacious living room, the same one I had seen in the photograph. One of the bedrooms was consumed by a bunk bed, which the kids scaled in delight. I peeked into tiny bathrooms, looking as if they had been built for a ship, lined in cedar, with tiny windows mosaic-tiled in sea glass. I fell in love with the guesthouse, a separate building from the main house reached by a steep flight of steps. Its chocolate colored rough-hewn exterior planks and light blue trim mimicked the main house and inside its yellow bathroom and whitewashed bedroom reminded me even more of the cottage in Quebec. I stood on its tiny deck and peered out at the sandy beach below, the Puget Sound a crystal clear aqua in the bright sun.

"Oh-oh," I said to J.R. "I think I've just become your emotional buy."

I spent the weekend calling my family, assuming they would talk me out of such an impulsive and expensive purchase. "Oh, Ab, it will be great!" my sister said unhelpfully. "It will be a place where we can make memories for the kids! It's going to be amazing! You *have* to do it!"

"You can't go wrong with beach-front property," my father told me in his best real-estate-expert voice. "They aren't building any more beaches." I couldn't argue with him. "If you can afford it, I think it will be a sound investment."

My financial advisor was my last hope, the one person who held the reins of my finances, the last voice of reason. I told her about my ideas for the house—hosting small writing retreats with different authors and healing retreats for the newly widowed.

"Abby, ever since I have known you, you have wanted to help others. I think this is in perfect keeping with your vision. I think it's wonderful. Don't worry about the finances. We'll work it out."

On Sunday afternoon, I toured Deirdre, Jack and Michael through the house. I felt like I was newly in love, and introducing my lover to them. They were infected with my passion. Another couple, we were told, had spent four hours in the house earlier in the day, and they seemed serious. I knew I needed to act and so after our tour, I signed a not-quite-full-price offer. By Monday afternoon, despite a competing full price, cash offer from my unknown competitor, the seller, who had been apprised by J.R. of my philanthropic plans for the house, told me that if I was able to increase my own offer to full price, they would accept my bid over the other offer. In astonishment, I complied.

On the day I closed on the house, I sat in an old, white-washed, egg-shaped wicker chair on the deck looking out across the water to the Olympus-like Mount Rainier, floating off in the distance thinking of Betty, admiring the view that she too had once admired. I longed for Arron at that moment, imagined sitting with him, silent in reverence and remembered the sign with his name, the two r's and the arrow pointing down the hill towards this house, pointing me, as he always did, it seemed, in the direction I was meant to go.

Lessons Learned (And Still Learning)
by Peggy Nagae

HAWAII WAS A TURNING POINT FOR ME, a significant emotional event, not just a celebration of friendship or even a remembrance of my friend, Kumi. Little did I realize, I would learn some of my toughest life lessons there: slowing down, being still, and taking time for me. My friend Kumi was right: my external focus on more clients, more money, and more production meant days flew by and my life's focus had become meeting the next deadline, rather than living mindfully and with an open heart.

Hawaii started out as a celebration of twenty years of friendship for LueRachelle, Lonnie, and me. We had originally met as consultants on a diversity project in Seattle, and in many ways, we were quite different. LueRachelle came from a family of educators who, as African Americans, were forced to live in segregation despite their advanced degrees. Lonnie is Caucasian, gay, and tall, and I am Asian, straight, and short, but our relationship also runs deep. We have had many long talks about our personal lives, and especially about our finances, love relationships, and spiritual views. As we often said, when Lonnie, LueRachelle, and I are together, we are the United Nations of friendship, different in background, similar in world view.

As I flew to Kono, I also had Kumi on my mind. Kumi and I had gone to the Big Island earlier in the year, when she had been in between chemo treatments for ovarian cancer. We had met over a decade earlier, as graduate students studying spiritual psychology. From the first day we went to lunch together, we liked one another, and from there our friendship grew and blossomed.

Kumi was born in Korea, raised in China and Japan, the oldest of many siblings. Her grandfather had been a scholar and minister in Korea; her father a doctor; her family, well-known and revered. When our friendship started, Kumi was in her late 50s and her 40-year marriage had ended. Kumi was a woman with backbone and heart. She was strong-willed, direct, and spoke her mind; at the same time, she was a seeker, committed to learning more about herself and others.

Ours was not always an easy relationship. We saw eye-to-eye on many things, but not on everything. She once told me "You work too much and worry too much about getting more clients and not having enough money." In my defense, I told her that by growing up poor, with Japanese American parents who had been born in Oregon, but nevertheless had been incarcerated by their own country during World War II, I had learned that getting an education, working hard, and being twice as good as a white person was how I would get myself out of poverty. Now being divorced, I had to make sure I saved enough money for my retirement. I did not tell her that my feelings were hurt, that I felt small from her comments, and that I was doing the best that I could. In other words, I did not allow myself to be vulnerable, to open my heart, and to share my feelings. We did not have the full conversation, like I *now* wish that we had had. Ah, regret.

But we also did have our *moments of truth*. One time, Kumi said, "I often do not share what I am thinking with you because I do not want to hurt your feelings and I know you will react defensively."

I replied with some feeling, saying, "You sometimes give me advice that I do not ask for, and it is challenging to hear."

After some silence, Kumi responded: "I think you are getting better at hearing."

"I am sorry that I make it tough for you to be honest with me," I said. I loved Kumi, even when I thought she was bossy and acted like the oldest sister that she was, and even when I reacted defensively, like the youngest sister that I am. And I know she loved me.

I was filled with memories of Kumi as I visited the places we had been to in Kona: the farmers' market, the shops along the beach, the mall where Kumi had bought a "shaved ice." In honor of Kumi, I bought a shaved ice and ate it at the same table where we'd sat. Back then, Kumi had been fairly vibrant and healthy, but her health started to decline several months later, and after enduring many cancer regimens and bowel obstructions, she made peace with herself and her life, ready to move on in her spiritual journey. In late November, she passed away in her sleep.

By good fortune, I saw Kumi the day before she passed. She was not conscious, but I sat beside her bed, holding her hand and expressing my appreciation for her love and wisdom. I apologized for the times I was stubborn and defensive and thanked her for loving me anyway. The next afternoon I received a message from her son, Miles, saying that she had passed.

Shortly after getting that message, I "saw" Kumi flying overhead and heard her laughingly say, "Whew, whew, whew." It was as though she wanted me to know that she was happy now, free of pain, and looking over me. Kumi's passing took a toll: even though I knew ovarian cancer was an uphill battle, I thought Kumi would somehow beat all the odds. For days and weeks, I was bereft about her departure. So many times I found myself wanting to tell her something and then would remember she was no longer reachable by cell. I had and kept our text, email, and phone messages. I could not bear to erase them.

As I was walking around Kono, I regretted not being a better friend, not dropping everything when she came to Montana that last time, not pausing sufficiently in her time of need. I did not tell her that I regretted not seeing her in August, when I was in Seattle on business and she had called me. I'd returned her call, told her I was in Seattle but was working. She'd wanted me to come over and see the purse she was making for me, but I was tired and it was late, so I said I just did not have the energy to drive from where I was staying to her house. I knew she was disappointed, and when I mentioned that Tai, my cat, was ill, and I was worried about him because I was leaving shortly to go to Bali, she said, "Sometimes our actions do not match up with our values." It stung, but I did not respond. Now, I wish that I had just taken my tired butt over to her house. As I thought about that conversation, I felt both tears and pangs of guilt for not doing more, being more, while she was alive.

Lonnie and LueRachelle had also known Kumi. Lonnie knew her through mutual friends, and LueRachelle through a trip that nine of us had taken to Turkey and Greece. I knew she would be proud of what we were doing: playing, taking time to celebrate our friendship. Among all her other advice, Kumi had said that I need to live in the now because you never know how much of life you have left: "Peggy, let's face it; we are all going to die, it's just a question of when, and how are we going to live."

Our days in Hawaii passed quickly. Lonnie loved the sun and was dedicated to getting a tan; LueRachelle had a report to finish but worked outside and was delighted with the temperature because it alleviated her arthritis. I started an electronic weight loss hypnosis course, read, and rested. On more than one occasion, LueRachelle exclaimed, "We need to stay for ten days; a week is *NOT* enough time." I agreed; not working was beginning to suit me!

We also spent time looking back over our twenty-year history and talking about old times. During one of our conversations, Lonnie mentioned a time when his partner, Bill, had to have surgery. He said, "Bill asked the doctor to talk to him during the operation, believing that it would help his healing process, and it did." I heartily agreed, thinking about the work I had done in hospitals and discovering that the environment of many operating rooms was toxic: doctors and nurses told dirty jokes, played loud obnoxious music, or were tense with each other.

On another day, we drove to Kilauea, thought to be the world's most active volcano. Going north, we headed into the mountains and to the town of Waimea. Again, Kumi came to mind. We had gone to Waimea's farmers' market together. Kumi had mentioned that her sister and brother-in-law had lived in Waimea, and I could see how they would enjoy this small town with its world-class hotels and golf courses, shopping centers, and best of all, a health food store, which Kumi and I had visited together.

Before we knew it, our time in Hawaii was almost up. LueRachelle once again said, "We need to spend more time here; at least ten days!" Unfortunately, that was not to be since the next day we would be heading back to rainy Seattle for Lonnie and LueRachelle and snowbound Montana for me. Lonnie decided to spend his last day lying in the sun. LueRachelle wanted to find a quilt show in Waimea. Not being a sun person, I decided to tag along with LueRachelle, curious to see how the pan-Asian Hawaiian culture would be expressed in their quilts.

Driving into Waimea, we found out that the show was scheduled for next month, and the date in the tourist guide had been a typo. We were disappointed, but thought we'd make the best of it by eating lunch before driving back to Kono. I bought a "lunch plate" of teri-yaki chicken and rice; LueRachelle got a mushroom burger.

While eating, I felt some pain in my chest/heart area. I thought it might be indigestion, so I stopped eating and drank some water. The pain persisted, so I drank some tea. Then I went to the restroom, thinking that might help. It didn't, but I chocked it up to heartburn and suggested we drive back to Kono.

Instead, LueRachelle insisted we go to the emergency room, where they took some tests, found nothing definitive, but said it might be my gall bladder. The doctor prescribed pain medication and was sending us on our way. Before leaving, I decided to call Carolyn, a friend, spiritual teacher, former nurse, and medical intuitive, who lived in Montana. I described my symptoms to Carolyn, and she urged me to take my symptoms seriously.

I told the receptionist I wanted to see the doctor again, and she sent us back to the same room. They ran more tests. Still not definitive, the doctor concluded I had some type of "bowel obstruction." They admitted me to the hospital, and I spent the night in pain, first getting morphine for relief, then asking for something even stronger. LueRachelle stayed right by my side, sleeping in an uncomfortable chair next to my bed. What a friend!

The next morning, I met Dr. Park, gray-haired and stately with a well-modulated, kind, strong voice. I assumed from his last name that he was Korean. Dr. Park explained that the obstruction hadn't resolved itself and surgery was required.

Panic set in; my head started spinning. I cannot remember his exact words when I asked what might be causing the obstruction, but I do remember hearing "tumor" and "cancer." The needle on my scare-o-meter jumped off the chart, and I wanted to cry.

When the nurse came to prep me for surgery, she asked where I was from. When I said Montana, she replied, "You look like a local girl." I gained comfort then, knowing I was in a culture where Asians were in the majority and knowing that my surgeon was Asian, especially Korean, because he reminded me of Kumi. I had never met her brothers, and certainly not her father, but I imagined Dr. Park was similar to them: competent, capable, and caring. I cannot remember if Lonnie's story of his partner Bill's surgery came to mind. I cannot remember if it was then that I asked Dr. Park if he sang, but something kicked in and out came my request: "Will you all sing to me during the surgery?" The nurses and doctor said, "Yes, we will!"

That was all I remembered until I was back in my room, and Dr. Park stopped by to tell me that the "bowel obstruction" had been my inflamed appendix. My fears about tumors or cancer went by the wayside, much to my relief.

When Dr. Park came to check on my progress a few days later, I asked him what song they had sung to me.

He smiled and said, "We sang 'Somewhere Over the Rainbow.'"

I have always loved that song, and now I had a reason for loving it even more. I thanked Dr. Park for singing, and he said in his modest voice, "You're welcome." Some weeks later, my dear friend Jennifer emailed me the Hawaiian rendition of "Somewhere Over the Rainbow" by Israel Kamakawiwo'ole, which is even more lovely than the versions I had heard.

I did wonder why I had gotten sick in Hawaii and had had the operation in Waimea. In turn, I could not help but think about the connections to Kumi: her sister and brother-in-law lived in Waimea; Dr. Park is Korean as was Kumi, and very stately, as I imagine Kumi's brothers are and her father was. Dr. Park's qualities also reminded me of Kumi: competent, alert, and wise.

Thank the Lord LueRachelle had stayed and not returned to Seattle on our original itinerary. She said she would stay and fly back with me, when I was well enough to fly. She did take the time when I was in need, without any hesitation. I teased her and said, "You will get your ten days in Hawaii, but probably not in the manner you thought."

She looked at me with her big eyes, saying, "Yeah… be careful what you ask for!" What a great friend! Lonnie felt badly that he had to leave, given he was facilitating a retreat the next weekend. It was what it was meant to be, for each of us.

It was not until I returned to Montana and had a session with Carolyn that I learned more about the spiritual whys and wherefores of my experience. Once I got back, I had to stay put in Montana. I could not lift more than fifteen pounds, so even at home, I was not doing any "heavy lifting." Instead, I slowed way down, slept long hours, and walked very slowly. I even sat and looked out the window at the snow, with nothing else vying for my time or attention. I experienced being present and in the moment, the things Kumi had urged upon me: slow down, don't work as much, play more. There she was again, in my thoughts, in my heart.

Kumi and I had talked about my spiritual purpose, and Carolyn and I had had many talks about my struggles with it, given the "armor" I had encased around my heart, the tyranny of my mind, and my perceived need to be tough in order to be taken seriously. Kumi did understand that need to be tough. We once talked about her having cried only twice about having cancer and she rarely discussed her cancer, let alone her feelings, with her family.

In fact, Kumi and I both struggled with allowing our true feelings to surface, and often we would rather stay in our heads. We talked about how difficult it was to even know what we were feeling, but she had been steps ahead of me on that path. In the six months prior to November, especially, Kumi had gently invited me to share with her and to be her best friend. I had not done such a great job of that and during my recuperation, I reminisced about what I could have done. I felt pangs of guilt for not making more time to be with her. But when I dug deeper, I realized my bad feelings were not so much about the time spent, but more about me being unwilling or unable to let down my guard, to open my heart, to be vulnerable with her.

I was protecting something that I cannot now remember. It is in retrospect, however, that I wish I had heeded Kumi's admonition sooner and been able to get there with her, while she was still physically present, rather than learning these lessons after her passing. I can now feel more of what she saw: vulnerability as a strength and opening of my heart, which means opening up to my vulnerability rather than seeing strength as a tough mind, a forceful personality, and a loud voice.

Now, I am learning that by slowing down, I can experience the preciousness of life that Kumi was talking about. Through my daily walks in the snow, taking time for meditation, and listening more fully and deeply when someone is talking to me, I have begun to feel the sweetness of life, rather than the franticness.

I am beginning to understand what Kumi was trying to teach me. *Now*, I feel that the best way I can honor Kumi's passing is to open my heart—a vulnerable heart—and honor myself, my True Self. In that way, I can become all that I am. And as I do that, I carry Kumi inside that beauty, my beauty. Thank you, Kumi, for leading the way; I follow gratefully in your wake.

My Stroke of Good Luck

By Jean Engler

I AM VERY INDEPENDENT AND I DON'T LIKE TO ASK FOR HELP. I also don't like to draw attention to myself. All that changed on Wednesday, February 25, 2004, when I was hit with a stroke of good luck.

The day started as an ordinary work day. I got up before it was light, showered, found something to wear, ate breakfast, and walked three blocks to the vanpool to work. At the office, I began my routine of turning on my computer, getting coffee, and starting paperwork. I was a paralegal for a cell phone company in the E911 department. This is the department that works with public safety answering points to locate a cell phone caller for the 911 system. It was a boring job but had the potential impact of a million dollar fine from the FCC if I made a mistake, so I took my work very seriously.

About mid-morning, I felt like I had been hit by a massive cold bug. My throat hurt and I had trouble swallowing my coffee. A wave of fatigue came over me like I had never felt before. I wanted to go home, but didn't have the energy to get a cab. I didn't want to draw any attention to myself or make a big deal about it. There was a little voice niggling at me that this was something major. I ignored it. I was so tired. My eyes kept drooping shut and all I could think about was lying down. The day, of course, dragged on.

Finally (it seemed like a week later), the van arrived at the front door. It took a Herculean effort to haul myself up into the van. I suppressed the urge to tell Patrick, the driver to go faster than usual on the way home. I did not say anything and did not participate in the usual banter about TV shows and movies.

About three quarters of the way home Patrick asked, "Why are you so quiet? Are you mad at us?"

"No, I just don't feel well."

"Sorry."

As we neared our drop off point, I asked Patrick to drop me at my house because I don't think I could manage walking the three blocks to my home.

I collapsed on the couch and fell asleep. I knew something was wrong and that I should go to the doctor, but I was in denial and I told myself I didn't have the energy. As the hours passed, I knew something serious was wrong but bargained with myself that I would go to the doctor in the morning if I didn't feel any better.

At first light, I knew I had to keep my part of the bargain. When I looked in the mirror, the left side of my face was drooping slightly and my fingers were numb. I went back and forth about driving myself but thought if I was hospitalized, what would I do about my car? Also, I knew I would get too much crap from my friends. I showered and took a cab to the hospital emergency room.

When I got to the ER, a bored looking receptionist glanced at me, then handed me a half sheet of paper to fill out. Since I came in under my own steam, was not obviously bleeding, and didn't have any bones pushing through my skin, I guess she assumed it probably wasn't very serious. The questions on the paper were:

Are you having any chest pains?

Are you having difficulty breathing?

Reason for ER visit today _____.

I wrote down 'possible stroke' and handed the paper back to her. When she read that, she acted like she had been hit with a cattle prod and jumped into action. I was hustled into a room, with a nurse flying in the door within 15 seconds. The next thing I knew, I was on a gurney and my vitals were taken. I was rushed to radiology for an emergency CT scan. It took a half an hour, but that's rushing in hospital time. Then I got the news—I had indeed had a stroke and would be admitted.

At this point, I felt relief. I was being taken care of and that I hadn't imagined my illness. I called my sister, Carol, and left a voice mail. I also called my friend, Jann, who worked at the medical center; I knew she would alert the girlfriend network. My friends were a very important part of my recovery.

I was taken upstairs to a semi-private room where I was poked and prodded and quizzed. My sister hadn't called me three hours after I left a message and I was perturbed that she wasn't checking her voicemail. It turns out she was out on a sales call with her boss, in her car, and when she did listen to the voicemail she said,

"I have to drop you off at Southcenter. My sister's had a stroke and I have to get to the hospital. Your wife can come pick you up."

In the meantime, Jann, came into my room to check on me and get information to pass on to the other girlfriends. She also let me know that our friend, Paulette, had been admitted to the hospital and was in the room next door.

Finally, my baby sister arrived. She was out of breath and flushed as she rushed into the room. I assured her that I was not dying, at that moment. I told her the bad news: she had to call Mom to let her know what's going on. She didn't want to but she called anyway. I knew it would be too difficult for me to call Mom. As I suspected, Mom said that she and dad are getting in the car to come to Seattle. Carol handed me the phone. Mom needed to hear my voice to know that I am okay. I tried to reassure her that I would be fine, but as soon as I started to talk I began to cry. It doesn't matter how old you are, when you are sick you still want your mom. I told Mom that she and dad didn't need to come out yet, we were still in the process of finding out what would happen to me. I was not in critical condition and I needed to get more information before they should make the trek out. However, she had already lost a child and worried that she would lose me. I told her that I would call her every day.

My two brothers were planning to meet in Vegas for the weekend with their girlfriends for the Lebowski fest. I didn't want them to worry and ruin their weekend fun. My youngest brother, Dan called me and I reassured him that he should go and have a good time as I was getting good care. My brother Paul did not call. I didn't expect him to, as we rarely talked on the phone.

The first night was rough. When evening fell, I was alone and scared. Every time I started to fall asleep, I coughed and woke up. This went on all night. I felt bad for my elderly roommate. I found out in the morning that she was partially deaf and slept through it all.

After hours of restless anticipation, the doctors finally made their rounds. They told me that I had a rare brainstem stroke and I was suffering from Wallenberg Syndrome. One of the positive aspects of this type of stroke is that the patients often recover fully. However, the main symptom of this syndrome is difficulty or an inability to swallow.

At this point I hadn't eaten or had anything to drink for three days. I am not hungry. Everything is surreal. I feel fine, not debilitated in any way. Actually, I feel a little too perky and I can't sleep. I can get out of bed to use the bathroom and shower, and I take my IV pole and go visit my friend, Paulette, who is in the next room for some tests. She tells me she heard me coughing in the night and is worried that I am not ok. I can't sleep and neither can the people within hearing distance. At the time I expected this to be fixed within a week. No one had told me yet what the healing process would involve or what the recovery timeline would be. The staff was still in discovery mode —running tests and trying to make sure I was stabilized. Explanations would come later.

On Saturday, I sent Carol to my apartment to pick up a few things for me. When she went inside, she was scared out of her wits by my brother Paul and his new girlfriend, Michelle. Instead of driving to Vegas from Montana for their fun weekend, they drove to Seattle so Paul could make sure I was all right. Of course, he didn't tell anyone they were coming. They visited me in the hospital and then left the next day. Paul just had to see me to make sure I was going to be alright. I felt good knowing I could lean on him if needed.

My other sister, Julie flew in from Albuquerque the following Monday to stay with me. I can't drive, or swallow, and I was acting goofy. She was not working so she could give me her time. For some reason I sent a message to people at work that I would only be off for three weeks. When I told my sisters, they rolled their eyes and said "OK." I could tell they were being patronizing but I didn't know why. I later found out that I kept insisting I was ok and didn't need any help. I was glad that Julie was there, but I believed it was only going to be for a visit. I could take care of myself.

My physician finally told me what I could expect for the coming weeks and months. I would need a feeding tube for nutrition, medicine and hydration. Watching hospital dramas on TV did not prepare me for the process of getting a feeding tube. The blonde lying on the bed with a small tube up her nose with perfect hair and makeup is not the reality. It took two nurses two tries to get the tube through my nose, down my throat, and into my stomach. I felt like I was being tortured. Oh, and the tube was bright yellow. Apparently, they didn't want anyone not to see it.

When I was released on Tuesday, after seven days in the hospital, it started to sink in that I might have a long recovery ahead of me. Once I was home it was difficult to do anything. I was extremely tired and could not concentrate. I made an appointment to see a rehabilitation doctor and a speech therapist to get my swallow back.

During the first few weeks I had vivid dreams as my brain worked to rewire itself. I woke up in the middle of the night convinced that Julie was trying to kill me. I thought she had hooked me up to my feeding machine and left me alone to die. I am so mad at her, but her plan fails I am still alive! It took me awhile to finally realize it was a dream.

I fell asleep to a story on TV about Princess Diana. I woke up convinced that I had been abducted by the royal family and they cut my feet off. I woke up as I was trying to figure out how to walk with prosthetic feet. Perhaps they were talking about Diana's work with landmines on the program. Another night I dreamt that Canada had given me a citation for breathing incorrectly. The dreams felt real to me.

Liquid nutrition and water was what I subsisted on since I couldn't swallow anything. All of it was put through my feeding tube so I couldn't taste how bad the formula was. Medication had to be crushed and put into my feeding tube. It was a messy job, but Julie didn't complain. I was getting weaker and I was in constant pain. The only time I was comfortable was lying on my side. We assumed it was a side effect from the stroke. I felt helpless as I slept a lot and depended on my sisters do everything for me.

I made the visit to the rehab doctor and found out I would be off work for three to six months. That's when I began to realize that my life had really changed.

Swallow therapy didn't provide any better prognosis. They told me it could take six months before I could swallow again. My new life consisted of therapy three times per week and it kept getting harder instead of easier. At that point I'd lost about thirty pounds. However, the pain in my side kept getting worse. I made an appointment to see the gastroenterologist to have a feeding tube inserted into my stomach and remove the nasal tube - which was affecting my ability to get modeling jobs. Plus, it's uncomfortable and embarrassing to be in public with a bright yellow tube coming out of your nose.

My friends stopped by frequently to visit with me, but the constant stream of visitors would quickly wear me out. I am never comfortable now and feel like I am getting worse. It was easy to blame everything on the stroke. When I visited the gastro doc he explained the procedure to me and said that sometimes there is a blockage and they can't insert the tube.

When he examined me he asked, "Is your stomach always this distended?"

I said, "'Yes," embarrassed that he commented on how fat I was.

When I got into the procedure room the next day, I was given some drugs to relax me. I felt a warm feeling, listened to some conversation, and the next thing I knew I was in the recovery room. My nasal tube was still there! After coming around and getting dressed, I went to meet with the doctor and my sister.

Julie and I were waiting in his office when I told her, "I think I sang Moon River to Dr. B."

"What?" she giggled.

When Dr. B comes in Julie asked him, "Did Jean sing Moon River to you?"

Dr. B said "Yes, and she was on key."

Then he said they couldn't get the tube in because there was a blockage. So I was sent to radiology for a CT scan.

That night we got a call from Dr. B with the results. As I watched Julie's face go very serious, I knew the news was not good. She hung up and took a deep breath.

"They found a large mass and you need to make an appointment with the surgeon on Monday."

Once that I knew there was something foreign in me, I wanted it out immediately. Monday can't come soon enough. I made an appointment to see the surgeon. She tells me she is pretty sure it is a benign cyst. The bad news it is the size of a watermelon and needs to come out. I left the office pretty shaken. Julie had gone home by this time, and Carol took me to the visit. Surgery is scheduled for the following week. At this point I knew there is no holding my parents from coming out.

My folks came out from Montana the day before my surgery. They were very worried. I was grateful for the support. Early the next morning, Carol picked us up for the ride to the hospital. We sat in the surgery waiting room before they called me in. I was calm, but uncomfortable at this point. I just wanted it to be over.

When I came to, I had an incision stretching from my breastbone to my navel that was stapled shut. There was pain, but an IV of Fentanyl soon took care of that. And, lucky me, I still had my nasal tube. I had to wait another day before the feeding tube that was put in my stomach during surgery could be used and the nasal tube removed. Small steps.

After I was moved to my room, my family came in to make sure I was alright. I shrugged off my mom's offer to stay the night. When it came time for mom to go home for the night, I asked her to stay. Once again I realized that it doesn't matter how old you get, when you don't feel good you want your mom. I was finally able to get a good night's sleep!

Other than the pain, I was so relieved to have that thing out. My recovery from the surgery took about a month before I was able to move around pain free and with my former grace.

The stroke recovery took a full three months before I was able to resume driving and a return to work. My swallow came back along with about 95% of the sensation on my left side. This was my stroke of good luck. I am not sure the cyst would have been found in time to prevent real damage if not for the stroke. I was so lucky this frustrating experience had a happy ending.

It also was the last time that I was able to have my Mom around when I was sick and that was a blessing.

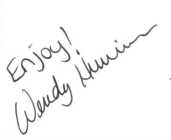
We're Going To Die

By Wendy Hinman

WE'RE ALL GOING TO DIE. SOMEDAY. Maybe even today. We all will. No one has lived forever. Not that we know about anyway.

But most of us live our lives as though there will always be tomorrow and spend our days in a mind-numbing routine, rushing through tasks on our to-do list. We become human doings instead of human beings.

Then something reminds us that our time here is limited, a serious accident, the loss of someone dear, or devastating news of a terminal illness. We never look at life the same way again. We stop to re-evaluate our lives and learn to focus on what is important.

The second year my husband, Garth, and I were married -- while we were still in that goopy, puppy-love stage that can so nauseate a jaded, jilted lover with lingering glances, over-enthusiastic delight in one another's cleverness, and excessive displays of affection -- we were in a nearly fatal car crash. We'd planned to drive from Seattle to San Francisco for Christmas, and when we awoke to icy conditions, we left anyway, even though the roads were almost impassable.

A few miles south of Portland, as Garth tried to keep our wheels aligned in the ruts the cars ahead of us had worn into the ice, a small white Toyota pick-up truck merged onto the freeway. When it reached the ice at the bottom of the ramp, the driver lost control and began spinning in front of us. I tried to remain still so I wouldn't distract Garth but soon our wheels lost traction and we also began to spin. "*We're going to crash*," I thought. I tried to relax, remembering how the main character, played by the teenaged hottie-of-the-hour Leif

Garrett, in an ancient movie had survived a horrible car crash because he'd been asleep.

I only know what happened next from what people told me later. We'd been T-boned by a double-tanker diesel truck on the only stretch of road that had any shoulder within miles. I heard Garth call my name from what seemed like another world. I felt soft fingers fish glass out of my mouth. I heard an authoritative female voice say, "Don't move her. She may have a spinal injury. Let's wait for the Jaws of Life." I wanted to tell them I was fine, but I wasn't sure if I was.

I don't know how long I'd been unconscious, maybe a few minutes. I opened my eyes as a mammoth metal contraption wrenched the door off the mangled car, which had been smashed to half its former width. Soon, I found myself surrounded by anxious faces as someone moved me on a gurney towards a waiting helicopter, its blades thumping in the frigid air. One face captured my attention: Garth. I will never forget his anguished expression as I whispered, "I love you" and squeezed his hand. It felt odd to have so many people witness this private moment between us and for a second I thought, "*How corny! Just like a cheesy made-for-TV movie.*"

The helicopter air-lifted me to Portland's Emanuel Hospital, leaving poor Garth to find his own way there. Evidently he'd survived the accident without injury and didn't merit a ride in the helicopter with me. Although I was the one on the gurney, all I could think about was how scared and worried he must be as we abandoned him on the frozen highway.

After an hour, hospital staff determined that I had no greater injury than a sprained shoulder and a concussion. They released me to Garth's care with firm instructions to watch for odd behavior resulting from the concussion. "You mean odder than usual?" he joked as he gently gave me a one-shoulder hug, relieved to have caught a ride with the wrecker to the hospital in time for my quick release.

My injuries would heal within a few months, but Garth and I were forever changed. The Christmas presents we'd carefully selected and wrapped, now sprinkled with glass shards, seemed irrelevant and silly. We couldn't bear to be apart. From then on, we did all our holiday shopping together, never again celebrating with the same frivolous spending. Our car accident had reminded us in our earliest days that quality time together was more important than anything else.

Time had become our most precious resource. Over the next few years we began to resent the demands our jobs placed upon us, as though they were our highest priority. We both worked long days, spent weekends running errands and sometimes felt like the fun of being together was eclipsed by workday responsibilities and outside demands. Searching for a way to regain control over our days, we saved carefully and discussed possible scenarios for changing our lifestyle.

As lifelong sailors, we struck on the idea of taking an extended sailing adventure to explore the world together. Within eight years we bought a small, simple boat that we could afford. As we simplified our lives, our friends wondered what we'd do for money. My BMW-driving sister-in-law, an attorney, accused us of being irresponsible because we wouldn't be dutifully contributing to our 401k plans. To secure the freedom to live jobless lives, we learned how to live on a 31-foot boat on $33 per day, the income that our house rent brought in each month. Yes, we lived in remote places, away from modern conveniences, without a car, a television, a cell phone, and even Internet access. But we had the luxury of time together. We spent our time doing things that didn't cost money: snorkeling, swimming beneath gushing waterfalls, hiking through the forest and using free wind to sail from place to place as best we could, even when it was barely perceptible.

Our sailing life wasn't easy. There were days when our boat rolled violently like a harpooned whale, when we plowed through walls of saltwater that soaked us through and times when we had to re-anchor our floating home in the middle of the night. We regularly hauled heavy backpacks full of groceries on foot in blistering tropical heat. There were many occasions when I had to remind myself how lucky I was, not only to be alive, but to *feel* so alive: to acutely experience both the good and the bad, often within the same hour.

We weathered typhoons and storms and we faced constant reminders of how little control we really have in life. We had days we thought might be our last, like the time we nearly lost our boat on a remote coral reef, or when a towering ship threatened to crush our home into kindling and plunge us into the icy north Pacific. I could not afford to move through my days on auto-pilot like I often had in my 9-5 life. Our continual struggle to survive never let us forget that we were alive. What made it all worthwhile was the time to appreciate each encounter as a gift.

As the saying goes, all things must come to an end. Three years ago Garth and I returned after sailing for seven years. While I could have sailed for years longer, Garth couldn't stand or sit properly in our tiny boat and was ready for a change. We never imagined we'd be gone so long or sail 34,000 miles, but we fell in love with the vagabond lifestyle. We loved being able to exert control over our lives in a way we hadn't when jobs, bosses and society dictated how we should live.

Readjusting was difficult. We'd missed so much while we were away: September 11th and the rise of TSA; an election contested by hanging chads and nearly the entire Bush era; the evolution of Skype, Facebook and smartphones; not to mention a reshuffling of NFL, NBA and major league baseball teams and players.

I could hardly cope with the frantic pace of life back home. Or the overwhelming choice of toothpastes. I could hardly bear to listen to the news. Perhaps being away for so long sensitized me to the overwhelming negativity of news reports. The hostile socio-political climate depressed me. While we had been away, the United States had broken into bitterly feuding camps, and the sniping was constant, ugly and counter-productive. Mistrust and demonizing others replaced tolerance. The poor and the homeless were no longer viewed as unfortunate people, but swindlers. It seemed like everyone was missing the point. In our years of exploring and struggling to survive, we'd realized the point of life wasn't to accumulate wealth or power or stuff, but to appreciate the gift of each day and make the most of it.

A financial meltdown stripped us all of the illusion of security, what everyone had supposedly been working toward. Nearly everyone's 401k plans were decimated; houses were no longer worth what people owed on them, and much of their hard-earned money gone. Ironically, what my sister-in-law worried would happen to us when we stopped contributing to our 401k plans happened to everyone despite their best intentions and careful sacrifice. Time didn't translate into money but instead into lost opportunity. The saddest part is the time friends lost working jobs they deplored for funds that vaporized in the stock market crash. The stock market may yet rebound, but those years can never be recovered. Realizing that reaffirmed our commitment to choose time over money and to keep living simply.

Yet back home I felt lost, rudderless, like I no longer belonged. While Garth struggled to readjust to the working world, I felt his absence acutely, like I'd lost my best friend. I sunk into a deep funk, almost too overwhelmed to drag myself out of bed each day and go through the motions of living. I'd lost my zest for life. My beloved adventure had ended and I felt as though I had little reason to carry on.

Within six months of our return, two friends were diagnosed with breast cancer. One of these friends had toiled tirelessly at her company for over twenty years, often working evenings and weekends. I boiled with anger when I learned she'd been laid off shortly after she received her diagnosis. Within a year, another friend had a stroke at the age of forty. Seeing her fight to form words and use her hands like she had only days earlier jolted me like an electric shock.

I realized how grateful I was for the time Garth and I took to explore the world. The time we had to stop and talk with people in the places we visited and experience a different way of living. The time to rejoice in the beauty of nature with the wonder of small children and the deepening of our relationship from the challenges Garth and I had overcome as a team. Even though our life was sometimes hard, the rewards exceeded the sacrifices. I'd do it all over again. I felt blessed that our car accident had come so early as a clear reminder instead of a permanent loss and that I'd stopped to listen.

But I also realized that since we'd returned I'd forgotten how temporary life can be. My friends were struggling to survive, yet I was wasting time lamenting the end of my adventure, one so few ever get to experience. Out voyaging I had found it so much easier to live in the moment because each day and each moment was unique. But now that we were back I was taking life for granted, assuming I'd always have the gift of tomorrow when I hadn't bothered to stop and even appreciate today.

I already possessed the ingredients for my happiness. What needed changing was not my location but my perspective. I needed to focus on what I *did* have rather than what I didn't have. I needed to look for the good, the joy in each moment and appreciate what I had right in front of me. And once again, I am thankful that I didn't have to lose my friends to remember how fragile life is and to realize there's no time to waste.

All That was Lost

By Sue Wiedenfeld

MY BROTHER WAS ADOPTED BEFORE I WAS. He was the first light of hope for the couple, John and Rita, who could have no natural children. He was called Tommy, and he had beautiful, lightly tanned skin, exquisite green eyes, lovely thick, long eyelashes, glowing white teeth, and a strong body. He had an impish, fun, energetic, very boyish side to him. He was whip-smart.

It was a fall day in Seattle in 2010, and I sat next to a woman at the Apple store, who was also getting her computer fixed. I heard her talk about just having returned from Vietnam. I listened and quietly inquired, "I think you said you just went to Vietnam?"

Our eyes met. She looked interested in my question. "Have you been there?"

"Oh, yes. I loved it."

It seemed like the light conversation of world travelers. We talked about the beauty, food, and people as we both wrapped up our business at the genius bar. She asked me how I happened to have gone to Vietnam. I thought about my brother. My beloved brother, who married his pregnant girlfriend at seventeen, then joined the service when he was eighteen. He was stationed in Vietnam where any tiny thread of childhood he had left was completely destroyed. The hundreds and hundreds of men on the navy vessels developed a culture of their own to survive the pain of the war: the pain of being away from their families for months on end. Many sent their money home to the families they loved. To survive and still provide for his family, my brother set up a money-lending business. The money he made let him survive by going on shore, where there were drinking, drugs, and women. Vietnam was where he moved into the shadow of his life. Where the emotional hell hole of war swallowed him.

Yet, he was the father who provided for his family. Years passed. He would and could never go back to the life he'd known before it all got so complicated. He no longer knew how. He was honorably discharged from the service. And then, he had the daunting task of returning to life in America and the family who really knew nothing about what he had been through.

I thought of all this as the woman I met in the Apple store waited to hear how I happened to go to Vietnam.

"My brother had been in the war. I had to go to the place where it happened…"

Her eyes were soft, understanding, as we stepped back from the counter, sharing in this deepest of ways.

"I had to see it for myself, to meet the people, to know and maybe begin to understand the country or the war in a different way."

"Did your brother make it back?" she asked.

I hesitated. "He came back, but his life was ruined. He was never the same. He was a casualty, not counted."

She seemed to understand as I asked her how she happened to go to Vietnam. She then told me details about her 'golden boy' brother, an only son, a fighter pilot in Vietnam, who had died instantly while saving another pilot weeks after going to war. Their family had never recovered. She had dedicated her life to a program for removing land mines in Vietnam, her way of coping with the devastating loss of her brother.

We stood together in the Apple store, connected by our understanding, our sad and terrible knowledge of each of our losses. I could hardly speak, swimming in memories as I said goodbye to her. She said it had been an auspicious meeting, our coming together this day in this way.

I was the other adopted child, who also held promise. Big, brown, inquisitive eyes. Golden hair. When my brother and I were four and five years old, we shared the pain of the loss of our adoptive mother. In our lives, my brother and I were together, and we were alone. I searched outwardly, as did he. I sought approval through doing well in school and later being in student government. He sought approval through the love of his girlfriend. And now, we are the same, reflecting on our lives, though we took different paths. He is wise, in a very world-seasoned way. And I have been searching my whole life. We have found different things, and we have found some of the same things: what truly matters, the importance of family connection. We share our yearnings. We love each other.

In our young lives, we connected deeply through the death of our adoptive mother and then, nine years later, when we were teenagers and our father was very ill, we decided together that he just couldn't die.

It was June 17th, 1967, almost Father's Day. I was 14 years old. It was sweltering hot in the California Central Valley way where 110 degrees is not uncommon in the summer. I had visited my adoptive dad in the hospital for what turned out to be the last time, just the week before. I was still feeling so strange about my visit. Dad and I had always been close. I had been the mascot for his basketball team when I was four. All my life, he had been easy to talk to. Even these last months when he had been so sick, I could sit on the edge of his bed in his bedroom and tell him about how much I hated wearing white polished saddle shoes to school when all the other kids wore tennis shoes. He would listen carefully, seeming to understand. He would tell me that he had had to wear clothes his mother made when the other kids wore 'store bought' clothes when he was thirteen, and somehow I would feel better, even when I still didn't get to wear tennis shoes like the other kids.

Around Christmas, he had told me he might die of his metastatic lung cancer. He was only forty-three years old and lying in our living room on the black and grey nubby couch we had always had, and which had always been covered with a brown throw with funny spongy stuff on the back and fringe. It had never looked right, always messy and misfitting. He looked pale lying there. I sat next to him on the green footstool with the worn piping.

"Sue, I may not get better. You know Mrs. Prandini died. It is very sad when a parent dies and they can't be with their family to see them grow up. I don't know why God took Mrs. Prandini, and I don't know if God will take me. There is nothing I want more than to see all my children grow up."

He was very gentle. Very real. He could see that I didn't even want to consider what he was saying. He was trying to let me know that he already knew. He was trying to be such a good dad, to warn me, to let me have some time to get used to the idea of his dying, to let me think the unthinkable.

I wouldn't hear of it.

"Dad, no, no, you can get well. We won't give up. There must be some medicine that will help you. We have to keep trying."

My eyes burned and I couldn't swallow. I could feel his gentle strength, the strength I loved, the strength he was trying to impart to me, his daughter he loved and didn't want to leave. I couldn't imagine life without him—even for a moment.

"I know sweetie, but it may not work. It isn't right, but it may happen."

He made it sound like it was a possibility, but not a certainty. In my heart, I clung to the uncertainty. At the same time, I felt like screaming "No, no, no, no, no! This cannot be! I won't let it!" Tears streamed down both of our cheeks. He gently welcomed me to him by reaching out his arms and, as I knelt next to him on the floor, he pulled me forward, hugging me tightly. I rested my chest on his chest and felt the warmth of my father, *so very alive*. My strong, loving, kind father. I rested my head on his thin shoulder, feeling the bones through his light cotton t-shirt. He bent his hairless head toward me as we both released the tears that had been longing to escape. Since he had said "maybe I will die," we could both cry about the possibility.

Together.

Even as I held tightly to the hope that somehow, some way, it would not happen.

Two days later, on Father's Day, he died. My brother's and my decision hadn't been strong enough to save him. And our world with my father was gone forever. In time, I learned to live a life without my father, remembering what he taught me about the moment, the only thing you can be sure of.

Seven years later, when I was twenty-one, I began searching for my biological mother. It took me nine years to find Phebe. I also found and came to know her children, my half-siblings, two sons and a daughter. In the twenty-six years since I had met her, the second son, Pete, and I had became close. I got his text in Seattle at 7:18 in the morning. My seventy-five-year-old biological mother was suddenly failing.

Phebe had been in a nursing home in Pennsylvania, near Pete, for three years by then, gradually declining. But this was an unexpected surprise. I cancelled my ten-hour work day, made arrangements with my husband and fifteen-year-old son, and began preparing to fly East see Phebe again while she was still alive. I made a reservation for a 3:05 p.m. flight.

As I sat on the plane, our lives together and apart flashed before me. The nine years of searching that left me fearing I would never meet her. The angst I lived with daily, knowing she had used a fake name on the birth records. The incredible and improbable experience of meeting her through a psychic when I was thirty, then meeting the family and seeing them all at different events over the years: My half-brother's weddings, my wedding, recently Phebe's husband's funeral. Feeling how much she had already seemed gone as her dementia had worsened. Remembering her talking about her mother's early-onset dementia and how it had continued over the years while her children were growing up.

I went into her room, saw her lying on her bed, oxygen on, and let the picture sink in. Walking around to the far side of the bed, I leaned down and kissed her forehead, slowly, gently. The room was quiet except for the sound of her breathing, the oxygen flowing. Open glycerin swabs were sitting on her night stand. Her lips looked parched.

I told her everything. Quietly. I thanked her for our life together. I thanked her for seeing and answering my ad in the personals. I thanked her for what she had given me: my skin, my hair, and maybe my personality traits. A chance to have a family that was able to raise me, when she couldn't as a nineteen-year-old college student. I told her how much meeting her and knowing her had meant to me, how much it had filled a hole in my life. How much I treasured our connection together and how I always would. We would always have that. She lay there, occasionally squirming.

I felt sad watching her. It made me think of all that we had experienced together, and all that we had not. I flashed on the time she came to visit my husband and me when we were at our cabin waterskiing. I remember, though I was thirty-eight then, a strange yearning to have her watch me ski, as a young child might ask their mother to watch them perform or play a sport.

We had skipped all that. We had met long after the days of "watch me" were over. We connected as two adults. And yet, we felt deeply our connection as mother and daughter, she forty-nine, me thirty at our first meeting. That day we sat at her kitchen table comparing our wrists and hairlines, sharing a glass of wine. I heard my family stories for the first time.

The years passed. I had a son. When he was three, he and I went together to her 65th birthday party at Pete's house, and she had just a few hints of the dementia that had so burdened her mother's life; she had become a bit forgetful in small ways. And now, at seventy-six, she was as her mother must have become: closer and closer to the end stage of losing her mind. No longer able to walk. Incontinent. She occasionally said a word that made sense. Mostly she had seemed to struggle, and it was sad to see her realize her struggling, as she tried to get words of any meaning out.

I had last seen her in November with my husband and son. I had seen her alone in October, just a month before that, and had stayed with her for the better part of three days, seeing her life, morning to night. We had a few interactions that allowed me to sense her usual kindness, her gratitude for my visit, and even her frustration with her inability to communicate. I often felt I knew what she was trying to say. Watching her struggle was painful. I would say, "Phebe, I know. Don't worry if you can't say just the right words. We are together and I know." And she would relax. And so would I. And somehow we actually did communicate.

Now, in what appeared to be my last visit, I decided to lie next to my dying mother. I got in her bed and we lay there, just breathing, together now as we had never been in fifty-six years. I put my arms around her and held her close.

I treasured this time in the night. This time alone, just the two of us. I told her some things out loud and others in my mind. I was revisiting all of our years together. I kissed her on her forehead several times. She slightly murmured, "Mmmmmmm," eyes closed, resting in her hot body.

"Phebe, I love you. I will be back in the morning."

It was 3:00 a.m. I decided to go to my brother's to get some rest. I left, time suspended, the night surreal as I made my way out of her nursing home and to my car, programming my GPS with Pete's address.

I arrived in his quiet, beautiful New Jersey suburb and found my way to his cul-de-sac. I parked, grabbed my things, and went to the open back door. I was alone, just me and the vast night sky.

I set my clock for 9:00 a.m. and went to sleep. When I got up, I found my half-brother waiting for me in his living room. We hugged, and he wanted to know how she had been, not surprised that there had been no real change.

We made it to her bedside by about 10:00 a.m. Pete stayed a while, then left to go to work for a few hours, glad to have me by her side. I lay with her again, savoring the warm body of our mother. Surprisingly, she did not have a fever this morning, though she was still unresponsive. I gave her our message with kisses on her forehead. "We love you and don't want you to suffer anymore."

By noon, the staff had cleaned her up for the day, but she seemed dehydrated. I knew she had had nothing to drink or eat since two days before, the day I had been called.

I decided to try to drip some ice water into her mouth, just a couple drops to moisten her tissues, instead of using the glycerin swabs. As I did this, she started sucking on the straw that I used to drip the water. Surprised, I decided to hold her head up and see if she would drink ice water from a straw. With her eyes closed, she sucked on the straw and drank the entire cup. A short time later, she drank juice and then even some Ensure*. Our "dying" mother seemed to be rallying.

By the time Pete came back, I shared the news. Neither of us quite knew what to think. We just didn't know. We would wait to see.

By that night, Phebe had begun to drink even more, and continued not to have a fever. It looked like she *was* rallying. She mumbled a few more sounds.

It was a strange time. A time of goodbyes, already said, and a time of reprieve;
this was not her time to go. We would have more time.

I stayed in her room late that night, very late, and decided to leave in the morning for an early flight home. Our best guess, and the doctor's, had not come to pass. We had been there, just in case. I slept on the plane, in and out of consciousness about Phebe's near miss. I felt complete, but not. It had been an ending of sorts, but then again, not.

I did let something go that visit. And I accepted something. Phebe's life is mostly over. At best, we may get a few more words or fleeting recognition. The timing of her physical surrender we do not know. We do still have some time to think about her and our lives with her.

And we had a chance to say goodbye.

Death in Four Days

By John Mace

April in Seattle changes so quickly; give it fifteen minutes and you'll have something completely different. It was spring, 1996, as I looked out through the seventh-floor windows of the hospital, observing a young man walking along the street below. An athletic young man, he moved with an attitude of self-indulgence and arrogance down the newly greening, shaded sidewalk. As I silently contemplated him, it dawned on me that I would never walk freely, unobstructed, unaware of the simple pleasure of breathing again. I would never feel the slant of the growing sun on my face, never detect the soft salty breezes blowing off the Puget Sound, or stroll with the ease of independence and innocence of thinking I had the rest of my life to be happy.

He ambled off out of sight and I was left to my silent revelation and tears. The oxygen continued to whisper through the tube into my nose, and other lifelines pumped and sucked heartlessly. I lay there in the crisp, white-bleached sheets, alone and overwhelmed at the realization that within a few days I would be dead.

Lying there bound by the tubes and suction machines, the feeling of losing control over my body had never been so intense. I think I'm like everyone else about this; I believe that at the very least, we have *some* control over our bodies. I never imagined that at age forty, I would be watching my body betray me. I couldn't breathe on my own, and my urine was taken from me automatically. Tubes delivered nutrients my body rejected; even water dripped like a leaky faucet into my veins. I felt so confined, restricted, and claustrophobic; never had

I been so vulnerable. Sometimes, I wondered if morphine was offered more to stop me from going crazy, instead of to numb the pain.

I had known for some time that I was exposed to HIV, so it came as no surprise when my diagnosis changed. Being emotionally present during this time of transition was important to me, and I had started preparing myself. Learning how to meditate and watch my thoughts had been a struggle. I had honed my skills at moderating my anxiety with positive affirmations. My health habits verged on obsessions with food, sleep, exercise, relaxation, and social connections. I had let go of my judgments as much as I could, and "forgave" myself for my many errors in judgment. Life and the pursuit of balance, being present with everything I did, became my mantra. Spirituality meant having a clear understanding of "God." It clearly was not traditional.

Maybe it was the natural endorphins, maybe it was all the previous self-work I had done seeking "God, The Tao, The Way;" I don't know. One thing was for sure; I was sleeping twelve to eighteen hours a day. It wasn't a sleep like every night… it was more than a dream, more of a journey. This "sleep" time was like a deep trance.

I'd travel to places that I'd never been, talk to people that were familiar and loving. I never had any fear. I felt a sense of excitement, freedom, and release. I was disturbed and sad when I returned. Once, I woke to my partner sitting beside my bed, and he turned to me with a look of puzzled relief.

"I wondered if you were already gone," he said with tears in his eyes.

"No, but I wish I were," I answered, reflecting on the experience.

I realized that the places and beings I was communing with were that "other" place; there were no judgments, no resentments, no guilt or shame, only intense overwhelming love and tenderness. There was an enfoldment of acceptance and joy. I remember the questions—not interrogations, but similar to "What did you learn?" and "How did you expand yourself? Who loved you and how did you love them?" Their intent was to share and celebrate the experience with me. I tried at times to share this experience with close friends, but the look in their eyes betrayed their disbelief. After a while, I kept my experiences to myself.

And so it was that eventually, time ticked away and decisions needed to be made as to how to proceed with my care. Doctors presented options, each one including an operation to open my chest to try to re-inflate my lungs. None of them was very hopeful. All of them said that I would probably be dead within four days. A time was chosen, Thursday—only days away—whereupon I would be lifted onto a stainless steel table and sliced open like a trout, exposing my lungs. Techniques would be attempted to re-energize my airways. Should all that fail, I would be taken to a room to live out my remaining hours. If God was merciful, I would die peacefully on the operating table. No heroic measures would be taken; DNR was the order, Do Not Resuscitate. The legal papers were signed; I was emotionally ready for this part of my life to end.

Over the next few days, friends and family would drop by unexpectedly. All of them wanted to express something but were not prepared or were unsure of how to verbalize the inevitable. No one teaches us what to say or how to accept our emotions as a natural part of life and death. When we are faced with those situations, we are ill-prepared to address them honestly and openly. Somehow, we expect that the dying will lead us with what to say. Many times it never happens, and the living are left to agonize with the words unsaid.

I had strengthened myself for this time; the only thing that mattered was love. I only wanted to hear the truth. The people that came to visit wanted to avoid the obvious and bring cheer, but I wanted to talk about the experience of dying. I wanted raw honesty. I wanted to know that my relationships made a difference. Many times I had to ask friends and family to leave, as I didn't have the energy to continue to hold the mask of ignorance any longer. Old stories of the past began to feel like a broken record that no one would stop. The past was dead. I realized how painful it was for me to let go of life. I had to consciously release all the binds that tied me to these people. I needed to grieve what I thought was the loss of my life. Yet, on some level, I knew that this was not the end, but rather a transition. My ego, however, wanted to hold on. I kept experiencing this conundrum, but my experience also was with the journey I took every time I closed my eyes. I felt so conflicted, as the people I loved wanted to be closer, but I needed to let go. The emotional pain was overwhelming me.

The intervening days passed with me in and out of consciousness, both living and dying. Being present and mindful was important to me.

The night before my impending operation was spent quietly with my partner and mother. I did not want any further attachments. It was hard enough to let go. I really didn't want to talk. I felt guilty because I simply wanted to be alone. I was preparing to loosen the final binds. Eventually, I asked them to leave, as I needed time to myself, to be with my experience, my thoughts, my grieving. A silence, a warmth, a dignity permeated my consciousness. I was alone. I felt a gratitude and appreciation for my life, for all the things I had experienced. I accepted all the events as lessons I had chosen on some level of awareness, even those that had caused my demise. I felt freedom in taking full responsibility for my actions. No blame, no guilt, no shame, only freedom. I was 100% responsible.

I did not notice the clock as its arms moved relentlessly toward the dawn. The sounds of the hospital evaporated in the fog of the mechanics and distractions of living. The surgeon knocked softly on the door, waiting for my response. I had been told he would be stopping by to explain what he hoped to do that morning. He looked hesitant and shamed. His eyes avoided mine as he spoke softly. He had studied my X-rays with meticulous scrutiny. He was an accomplished surgeon, and yet he couldn't seem to find a satisfactory solution to this problem. He was a man of science, and the problem seemed unsolvable to him. He spoke of the mechanics of the procedure, and I felt him struggling with the truth. Somewhere I wanted to help him, but I couldn't.

"You know, Einstein said that you cannot solve a problem at the level of the problem," I said with a reassuring voice.

He looked at me directly.

"I know that all will be as it should be," I mumbled.

His eyes watered. He turned and walked from my bedside. No further words would come.

The morning dawned early. A young man came to prepare my body. My mother and partner arrived. I knew what they were feeling; that they were saying goodbye for the last time. It's one thing to say goodbye to someone that has died traumatically, but another to let go as the person is still there. The heartbreak is beyond comprehension. The look of terror, hopelessness, and helplessness is normally reserved for situations of unimaginable horror. Yet, here in this hospital room, curtains drawn, machines echoing out minute electronic songs, I said goodbye to the first person I had ever known, my mother. Children are never supposed to die before their parents; it disrupts the natural cycle. Saying goodbye to my partner of ten years catapulted my emotions into an abyss. The tears streamed down their faces. Words were lost. Nurses filled the room and I was gently raised out of my bed onto a warm steel gurney. Every care was taken for my comfort.

I remember wondering what a condemned man thinks as he is being walked to the electric chair: does he regret his life, take responsibility for his crime, panic?

I watched the florescent lights move overhead, like street lights on a dark highway, as they pushed my body down the cool hallways toward the white-tiled operating room. As my bed rolled into the room, the surgeon approached and said he would do his best. He turned and walked into another room.

The nurses, technicians, and assistants seemed to be walking around mechanically, getting their equipment ready, but behind their diligence was a quiet cadence that moved to the rhythm of sorrow. I had met many of them before, so there was an acknowledgement of respect and humanness. I was honored by their compassion.

The room eventually settled into operation mode. Lights were illuminated, and the doctor that administered the anesthesia softly asked me to relax. A part of me, my ego, wanted to resist the entire experience, show that I could overpower the medications, but it was to no avail. I slipped behind the veil of consciousness.

As the sheets were placed over my body to create a sterile environment, I realized I was watching the dance! I was observing from above my body, silently, comfortably, aloof from the emotional dance unfolding before me. Time was missing, but I could hear and see all that was transpiring to my body! The choreography of slicing open my body seemed like someone cutting on a rare steak. My lungs were flattened like a chicken breast placed in a frying pan with a heavy weight lying on top. Hours must have passed as everyone tried with every skill they knew to re-inflate my lungs, but it was not to be. I watched as the surgeon struggled to hold his emotions steady as his knife. The hours and stress of the operation took their toll; he was drained. As the desperation of the situation bore down on the room, hope evaporated. Nothing could be done. Standing beside my body, I saw the surgeon look up in my direction, and I could see his blue eyes. He was remembering something. Then, with a movement that defied his professional judgment, he scraped the lining of my lungs and the other membrane of my chest cavity. He did this several times to each side. Then he motioned for them to close me up. He walked away. I was to be taken back to my room. The operation was a failure. Everyone was aware of the inevitable.

According to my mother, she and my partner were standing outside the recovery room when the doctor told them it was a failure. At first, they stood there shocked and numb. My mother sank into a chair and said a silent prayer to my dead father that she had done all that she could, and now it was up to him. The doors opened from the operating room, and my mother rushed to my side, whereupon she saw a look on my face that said I was "furious." She said she knew at that point, I would survive. My partner later mentioned that he had seen that angry look on my face before, when he thought I was dead and he had woken me from that "other" place.

I recovered slowly to the sounds of the electronic songs. Something had shifted inside of me. I still could not breathe alone, and tubes were in more holes than were natural, but I was different; a metamorphosis had taken place.

The scratches that the surgeon had made as his last attempt caused a scar, like a Velcro adhesion. The chest muscles acted like a low-pressure crane to slowly, via shallow breaths, millimeter by millimeter inflate the lungs with the help of pressurization. Within 48 hours, my lungs had started to inflate. A month later, I was released from the hospital to go home. Synchronicity must have been working in my favor, as were the new combination drug therapies I had begun. I was sent home with a bag full of medications that eventually rejuvenated my immune system and stopped all replication of the virus.

Life continued on, and I adjusted to the thought that I would be around to enjoy it. It was a hard transition to begin to have hope again, to plan for a future, to reattach to all those people I had slowly let go. Some of them I chose not to re-engage. I had learned that everyone has a path to follow, and ours had taken different directions. I rarely think of them any longer. It's not that we don't care about each other, but eventually we realized that the only thing that kept us together was a shared history. History is dead. For those whose company I sought out again, I was different and they could sense this.

To this day, I continue to deepen my understanding of the events during that time, practice meditation, expand my spiritual growth, and try to learn something new every day.

Caught

By Ashly Moore

I saw it the moment I walked into the spotless kitchen. My diary lay open on the table. A sense of exposure; a mental check—did I leave it like that? Who might have seen it? Moving closer, internal warning bells amplified as I spotted a yellow post-it stuck to the page with these words scrawled:

Ashly—you left this out. We need to talk. Aunt C.

The horror of my situation trickled into the pit of my stomach as I pulled the note off the page and scanned the words I had written that morning—a description of my recent transgressions.

… I've been doing things I shouldn't like sneaking out at night to meet Andrew. Things tend to get a little out of hand at 4 in the morning.

When I was sixteen I left home and moved in with my aunt and uncle in Salt Lake City for a few years. My parents lived 325 miles south in St. George, Utah. In our culture, when teenage girls suddenly moved away to live with relatives it usually meant an unintended pregnancy, but in my case this was not the reason.

The summer before my junior year, on a visit with family friends in Salt Lake, I met Andrew, my first serious boyfriend. I was in Love. Andrew wasn't like any of the other boys I knew. He was exotic and mysterious, with dark, Mediterranean looks, and a musical, poetic way of speaking. My resulting campaign to leave home was motivated entirely by my desire to be with him, though I had the sense not to say this to my parents. I talked about my general unhappiness living in St.

George and the isolation I had felt there since moving from Michigan when I was ten. Even though I was Mormon and the daughter of a successful surgeon – both status symbols in our small, insular society —I had always felt like a fish out of water.

Despite my passionate appeal, I didn't truly believe that my parents would allow me to move away. It startled me when they seemed to take it seriously, latching on to the hope that a new environment might help me tap into the potential that they believed I was wasting. I came from a family with high credentials, and so far my academic performance had been decidedly mediocre. My parents had been straight-A students and attended prestigious, east coast colleges, as had many of my aunts, uncles and older cousins. This was the expectation.

Aunt C. and Uncle G. were willing to take me in with the condition that I would serve as a positive role model for my younger cousins— perhaps as some sort of antidote for the hinted-at rebellions of their daughter Isobel who had just left home for her first year at college in Massachusetts.

Magically everything came together. As unbelievable as it all seemed, I would move away from my parents and six younger brothers and sisters. I would begin my junior year at Rowland Hall-St. Marks, a small private school in Salt Lake City.

After a whirlwind month of shopping, packing and other logistical preparations, my parents helped me load up my little blue Toyota hatchback and I drove five hours to Salt Lake where I took up residence with my aunt, uncle and cousins. The Raleigh family lived in a distinguished Tudor-style brick home in the upscale East Bench neighborhood. My aunt and uncle were impressive and well-respected. Uncle G. was a well-loved pediatrician, Aunt C., a judge. They had five children, the three youngest still living at home.

The Raleigh household was stylish, clean and ordered. My uncle was tidy and organized. He made plans and schedules, carrying his Franklin Planner tucked under his arm at all times in case he needed to retrieve information or write down an important note. He, more than my aunt, ran the household, preparing meals and managing children. This was a shift for me, having grown up with parents who embodied more traditional roles; Dad: Breadwinner, Mom: Homemaker. Each morning as I ate breakfast Uncle G. cordially informed me about the day's schedule.

"Ashly, we will be having dinner at 5:15. Stir fry. Will you be joining us?" It was endlessly astonishing to me that dinner actually happened at the predicted time and that each evening the family sat down together at a pre-set table and ate a pre-planned and balanced meal. We talked about our day and discussed acceptable and appropriate topics. After dinner, the dishes were quickly and effortlessly cleaned up by the adults as the kids retired to bedrooms for homework or relaxation. If done with homework, we might watch TV in the dedicated recreation room.

This environment stood in stark contrast to the typical evening in my parent's home, where there rarely seemed to be a clear plan or, if there was, any ability to adhere to it. Here's the kind of scene I recall from around that time: Mom remembers in the middle of making dinner that she forgot to pick twelve-year-old Sarah up from dance class. She rushes off, asking me to take the food out of the oven and get the kids fed. When the buzzer rings, I set the steaming casserole – a layered concoction of tortilla chips, taco meat and kidney beans, topped with cheese – on the counter with a shout, "Dinner!"

My brothers and sisters who are at home drift into the kitchen to fill plates, which they eat in front of the large-screen TV that dominates our living room. I position the baby's high chair so that she can watch too and sprinkle the tray with cheerios any time she squawks. I remember to give five-year-old Robyn her shot of insulin only because she reminds me. Sarah storms in angrily, having waited outside the dance studio for nearly an hour. Mom has remembered that she signed up to take dinner to an ailing older couple from our "ward" (the Mormon term for congregation) and is off to the grocery to pick up a roast chicken and some deli salads for them. Dad comes home, exhausted from a day of surgery. Deftly ignoring the clamor of quarrels and messes, he takes a plate to eat in front of his bedroom TV. Mom arrives an hour later to find dishes piled high in the sink and children sitting dazed in front of the TV. She asks me to help cleaning up and getting kids to bed, but I plead too much homework and escape to my room, where I don't actually do any homework.

The Raleigh home was a haven from chaos—safe, clean, and predictable—but at times it felt claustrophobic to me. Everything from the schedule to the environment was subject to an uncompromising sense of control, emanating from Uncle G., whose singular discipline often felt like a reproach. In addition to his success as a doctor, he was a respected leader in his church and community. On top of that, he was a nurturing father and husband, tirelessly serving his wife and children. It seemed an impossible example to live up to and I struggled with the urge to scratch at the veneer of perfection that he created. At times I sensed this same impulse in his children and even Aunt C. Within the predictable, orderly environment a sneaky tension lurked in tidy corners and peered out from underneath tasteful hard-wood furnishings.

It wasn't that the home I had come from didn't hold its own conflict. My parents' relationship lacked cohesion and the effect cascaded downward—an avalanche of unmet needs and chronic hurt. Our family unit often seemed like a ticking time bomb, threatening to burst apart, but in our case the tension was masked by chaos. Aberrant behavior in the Raleigh household was hard to miss, while amidst the bedlam of the Moore residence, mischief frequently slipped through the cracks.

Neither home seemed quite right to me. The bedlam of my own family found me struggling to hold things together and looking for escape, while the Raleigh environment of frozen tranquility gave me an uncontrollable urge to make waves.

I was, by far, the messiest person in my new home. Uncle G. frequently asked me to "please" try to keep my room tidier. When I prepared food in the kitchen I had to be reminded to clean up after myself. Things were rarely left out of place, which was why the sight of my diary open on the kitchen table meant certain disaster, and the measured reprimand of Aunt C.'s note filled me with dread.

The night before I had waited in my room as Aunt C. prepared a bowl of popcorn, her favorite bedtime treat. The warm smell wafted through the house and I heard her footsteps on the stairs leading up to her bedroom. Uncle G. finished his rounds in the basement where the younger kids slept. He said goodnight as he passed my room and followed Aunt C. up to bed. I waited for the sounds of their feet to stop moving overhead and then tiptoed through the darkened hallway and out into the icy, breath-fogged night, too excited to feel the chill. These illicit rendezvous had been happening about once a week. Usually we drove somewhere—a park or a diner—but that night, I climbed into Andrew's warm car and we pushed down the seats, kissing for a while, right there in front of the house. As his hands grasped at my shirt, I breathed in his scent, which was both familiar and foreign, a combination of wool and licorice. My fingers tangled in his tight, wiry curls. There in the steamy air of his tiny hatch-back, all I felt was the thrill—like fireworks in my chest—of being desired and having desire.

The next morning, sitting in the cozy breakfast nook of the kitchen, I thought about what we had done and enjoyed the shimmery tremors that ran through me as I remembered his hands and his lips and his rough chin. I knew that I ought to feel guilty, but I couldn't seem to feel anything but delight. Alone in the house—everyone else had already left for the day—I decided to confess my sins to the page.

Now, hours later, I knew I had been found out as I reread the words I had written, stark against the clean, pale wood of the kitchen table. The post-it note stuck to my finger and I had an impulse to tear it into bits. But struck with the knowledge that this was now a permanent part of the story, I placed it back on the page and closed my cloth-covered book (a recent Christmas gift from Mom), feeling suddenly irritated by its festive green and red pattern. Momentarily letting myself hope that she hadn't read it at all and that the note was about something else, I went to my room and lay down on my bed. I thought about how later, when we'd gotten too cold, I invited Andrew into the house. Thank goodness I hadn't written any of the details of what had happened then.

My jeans were discarded in a pile on the floor. Andrew's hands found their way up my shirt, fumbling with my bra. This felt bad – wonderfully so. Still the fireworks, but now they were pulsing through my pelvis and reverberating downward. He pressed his thigh between my legs and the sudden warm pressure against the thin fabric of my panties was too much for me, causing a blissful explosion. A taste like butterscotch seemed to fill my mouth as I struggled to stay quiet. As the delicious waves died down, I felt suddenly very tired.

"We should stop," I said, perhaps abruptly.

"Why?" Andrew asked pragmatically. "I don't want to stop."

"Well, if we don't stop, things will go too far."

"I *want* to go too far," he said, with a smile in his voice.

I felt thrilled by this admission, but shocked too. Pre-marital sex was strictly verboten in our world. Mormon kids might secretly want it, but we knew we should never admit to it. It was time for him to go. In my mind, I was being virtuous.

The truth was our relationship was starting to sour. I had reasons to suspect that Andrew was not someone I could trust. A few weeks later I would find out that he had been lying to me—dating other girls—and I would break it off. I would turn to my friend, Brandon, who was solid and straight, honest and kind—everything a good girl should want.

After walking Andrew to the door and pushing him out into the cold, dark night with a few more kisses, I fell into bed and slept, immediately and deeply. Luckily for me my classes didn't start until ten o'clock the next morning. I waited until everyone was gone before I got up. I ate my cereal alone in the quiet, clean kitchen and wrote in my journal before rushing out to school—late as usual.

Reading over the words that had condemned me, I could hear Aunt C. moving around upstairs. She was waiting for me to come and find her. With a sick feeling in my stomach, I got up, climbed the creaky stairs to her room and knocked on the door. She opened it with what seemed a smug expression on her face.

"Let's go and have a talk in the living room," she suggested.

We sat across from each other in uncomfortable chairs.

I waited for her admission. "So … you've been sneaking out," she said.

"I can't believe you read my diary!" I was freshly angry, even though I had already known.

"Ashly, you left it *open on the table*!" Her voice rang with exasperation. "I was just going to put it away for you, but I found it difficult not to notice what was written there."

You should have tried harder, I thought, but all I said was, "I don't think I would have left it open."

"Well you did! And considering what you wrote, I think it's possible that you left it out on purpose. That you wanted to get caught."

"I did not!"

"Well, regardless of whether or not you intended me to find out, I have, Ashly," a deliberate pause, "And there *will* need to be some consequences. We can't have you behaving this way while you are living in our home."

These words covered me in shame and I remained quiet for the rest of the conversation. Clearly I had no case, no solid ground to stand on. I was, of course, guilty. Aunt C. explained that my parents would be told and restrictions would be put in place. My actions would be closely monitored. I would not be allowed to sleep over at friends' houses for the time being. Another stipulation (suggested later by Uncle G.) was that I would be required to attend church every week. No more skipping.

The next few days involved uncomfortable phone conversations with my disappointed mother, followed by several months of probation, during which my anger mounted. The more I thought about it, the angrier I got. Aunt C. had no right to read my journal. How dare she punish me for something that she had no business knowing about? Her position as a judge seemed ironic. How could she not see the injustice she had imposed on me?

Before living with my aunt and uncle, I had harbored the belief that they were perfect. I had grown up hearing about their accomplishments from afar: their impressive careers; their beautiful, talented children. Living with them gave me insight into the heavy weight of maintaining this seeming perfection. But instead of making me feel closer to them, this only added to my anger. It seemed somehow dishonest for them to maintain this flawless façade—irresponsible even.

Anger was becoming a habit. My fury filled me with energy, liberation—a thrill, I couldn't admit to liking. In my car—my only truly private place—I would scream and curse, savoring the rush I felt. The authority had shut down my illicit behavior, but inside, I was collecting an arsenal of bitter fuel, a tinderbox filled with resentment and disappointment—Aunt C.'s invasion of privacy, Andrew's betrayal, my parents' dysfunction.

I was consumed with disillusionment and isolation. I rejected everyone and everything with a caustic rage. I felt that there was very little left in my life worth keeping. Perspective had revealed my own family's chaotic instability and I knew that wasn't what I wanted. Yet, I was certain that the pristine lifestyle of the Raleigh family was also not for me. I had rejected Andrew for the lies he told and now I was dating a trustworthy boy who, sadly, could not set off the fireworks.

Rejecting all of the realities available to me felt like self-annihilation. It was terrifying, but exciting too.

In retrospect, I can see that I was getting ready for big changes. In order to muster the energy to move away from the people and things I had known and loved, I had to build a bonfire fueled by my discontent. Everything I valued might be lost in the flames—yet, I found myself more awake and alive than ever before. I was poised for the next phase of my life—ready for my evolution. But I couldn't see it yet.

Pilates *"Practice"*

By Laura Hebert

"To keep the body in good health is a duty . . . otherwise we shall not be able to keep our mind strong and clear."

~ Buddha

"Look in the mirror, Laura; your legs are not parallel." My Pilates instructor, Pam, tells me how to perform the latest rendition of pretzel body torture. I'm on the floor on my side with legs stacked (apparently crookedly), poised to lift them together into the air, repeatedly. *It is only 8 a.m.–how can I be expected to do multiple gymnastic repetitions this early in the morning?*

Perky Pam (petite, well-toned, though not *too* skinny) gives her instructions with a drill sergeant's exacting measure. A true believer in the exercise guru Joseph Pilates' method of *"Contrology,"* she is determined to make her students increase the strength, flexibility, and control of their bodies. We are told to put our legs into "table-top" (this is lying on your back with bent legs up–imagine a praying mantis on its back). Then she proceeds to place an eight-inch fitness ball on our shins, asking us to roll our upper torsos towards our knees.

"Keep those abs tight! Don't let the ball drop. Head down, then up, twenty times." *Are you kidding me? There is no way, no how I can get up to twenty!* My legs wobble around but I do manage to keep the ball up.

My life feels like that fitness ball right now. I want to keep all things up and balanced but know that with the slightest upset it will all fall down. I am teetering, like this ball, between sanity and insanity, between staying and going, between all is well and all is disaster.

"Your lower leg is at four o'clock, Laura; it needs to be at six." Now she has us on the floor on our sides, doing forward leg thrusts. My 50-something overweight body does not comply gracefully to this command. *Don't you know I put my leg there because I cannot keep it at six and stay balanced!*

I find my mind wandering to our remodel project, the never-ending, apply-for-a-Guinness-world-record-for-the-longest-ever remodel, Phase Three, or is it Thirty-three now? *Must remember to get the electrical permit renewed.*

The renovation is progressing, it really is, I tell myself. Never mind that we moved into this house in 1988 and have been suffering the plague of being "do-it-yourselfers" to the extreme. It seemed like a good idea at the time to save money by doing most of the work ourselves on a new shop and second-story addition. Never mind that what was going to be just an add-on family room for our now-graduate-school-aged children has yet to be realized. I still keep thinking, *when the house is done, I will feel so much better and be able to focus on things I enjoy doing, like writing.*

"Shoulders down, Laura! It is important to keep your posture correct for the next move." It's Pam again, intruding on my reverie. *Why can I never remember to keep my shoulders down and do it right?*

Just this week, in mid-December, the windows were delivered. Surely this good news alone should carry me through the rest of the winter with the house not being finished, living in a confined basement space that serves as living room, kitchen, laundry room, and look, see, that's my sewing area in the corner by the utility closet! Waiting and waiting for the persistent bad weather to turn better before beginning the last (!) part of construction only requires my infinite patience.

Pam now has us sitting with legs straight in front of us, bending to touch our toes. She admonishes me to have my feet flexed, not pointed. *Why does it seem she is only picking on me today? Of course, she hasn't humiliated me* **too** *much, not like she did last week when she told Ann her feet stink.*

There are lots of small things to do before the last big push with THE PROJECT. I could figure out all the remaining electrical supplies that are needed. I could contact the plumber and figure out if we can use plastic instead of now-outrageously-priced copper pipe. I could paint the hallway in the portion of the house that is finished, *just to feel like we are progressing!* Somehow these things seem too over-whelming to accomplish right now.

In class we are on all fours now, doggy-style, and lifting legs, bent, one after the other, to the side. My face is scowling and I'm panting as I lift my shaking legs. *Holy crap, why am I doing this class anyway? It is way too hard for me!*

Further mind-wandering: my husband Tom has been so down in the dumps these past several months—mostly from the pressure at work that seems to be the norm these days—do more for less pay and quicker! Then his father passed away in November, and it seems his manly way of dealing with the grief is to spend any spare time he has turning bowls on the lathe rather than working on the house. These bowls, made of cast-off wood, are piled on any spare space left on already-crowded bookcases hugging the walls in our "temporary" living space. They **are** beautiful, but secretly I am annoyed and want to either break his lathe or leave him, permanently, with the unfinished-house mess. *But, you must let him grieve in his own way!*

She now has us on our backs, lifting alternate legs, then crossing them over, bending, extending, bending, crossing over. Now adding arms. Now closing opposite eyes. *I can't do that! I am the world's most uncoordinated human being, bar none!*

I'm reminded of a folk-dancing class I took in college, thinking it would be an easy PE credit. As soon as I'd gotten fairly confident that I'd mastered the schottische (a polka-like dance with a little hop dropped in) we switched to another dance, more complicated than the last, and I stumbled miserably across the gym floor. My ego suffered horribly—I was never picked to dance by one of the four guys in the class—and instant flashbacks to horrific middle-school PE experiences kept me from improving.

"This is so important for aging bodies, to keep 'the core' strong and in shape." Pam reiterates her main Pilates mantra, 'it's all about the core.' Unfortunately, my body refuses to acknowledge this admonition. *My core, my core? I feel like an apple core that has been tossed into the trashcan, chewed and discarded.*

My thoughts return to my middle-school PE experience: imagine a reeking, pubescent gym with the boys lined up on one side and the girls on the other. You were supposed to dance with the kid directly across from you. I, being at the end of the line, noticed that the dumpiest kid in the class was shoved to the end of the boys' line to go with me, in spite of the teachers telling us not to move around. Humiliated, I was matched up with Albino Boy, four inches shorter than my 5'2" and with hair so blond it was actually white and skin so white it was transparent. Albino Boy had feet that he had not grown into yet, which proceeded to stomp on my once-white Keds. I found that if I closed my eyes as we attempted to twirl around the floor (screech, screech, from the rubber on our shoes) I wouldn't have to look into his beady, pale-blue eyes. *God, let this hour be over!*

In Pilates class, we are on the floor again, on our backs, doing a further variation on the first 'ball torment' maneuver. Our legs are now straight in the air, and Pam places the fitness balls on our up-stretched flat feet.

"Come on, you can do it! Keep that ball up there! Ten, nine, eight," Pam counts downward. *My calves are twitching, you witch, I'm gonna drop the ball!*

If I can just make it through the winter, all will be well. Look, the windows are delivered; we **have** to finish the house—it **has** to get done! There is no other option here. We can't back out now with only half of the work complete. *Or can we?* The lazybones part of me wants to abandon all.

"Lift your legs off the floor, then your arms." On our stomachs, flat-out, we are told to do the impossible: teeter on our abdomens with appendages outstretched. *No, no, **please** not the dreaded dual-lift. You are giving us every hard one today, you Nazi!*

This is one of the most difficult exercises for me, and I'm only able to lift my legs about one-half inch off the floor. This seems to parallel the progress I'm making in getting along with my husband right now. We seem to be at odds repeatedly about getting the house finished— he keeps saying he loves 'the process.' I keep saying *I love completing things.*

"I AM NOT A BODY, I AM FREE."

Why this particular phrase keeps popping into my head during the course of the class today, I cannot say. It is a saying from a book I have read that ultimately espouses that we are not bodies; we are mind and can choose to think differently about *everything*. I am oh-so-far from being in a state of enlightenment and from even coming close to understanding such things. Just one day without pain while doing Pilates would be good for me. *Just one day without blaming my husband for everything that's not going right would be good.*

"Focus, Laura; roll over and look at me!" Pam is drawing my attention back to the room, the music, the movement, and our bodies. At first, I am upset that she should once again be pointing out my inadequacies, but then a quiet little comment pops into my stream-of-consciousness thoughts and says *be willing to learn.* Ah, yes. So true. I give up so easily on myself and my ability to learn. I want to blame Pam for being too harsh; I want to quit this too-hard class and my too-hard remodel project and my too-hard marriage.

We are nearing the end of the class, and we do some yoga postures to finish. While we swoop our arms up in a semi-circle on our tippytoes, Pam says, "Breathe. More. Suck in more, more, up, up, up!" *Do I have any more capacity in me? Any more room? Yes?*

"Wow, Laura; I do believe you are the most-improved student of mine this year," Pam says as we are leaving. I don't know whether to thank her or slap her—is this just a ploy, another way to get me to place my body in one more contortion beyond my abilities, next time, or a kind word said out of a sense of remorse for having criticized my sloppy technique throughout the entire class? I mumble a 'Thanks!' and vow to keep up with walks, with at-home weight lifting, and with all *positive* thoughts concerning the completion of the remodel.

As I walk home, I remember the first classes I took with Pam, over a year ago, and realize that I *have* made progress. Back then I refused to complete many of the exercises she assured us that eventually we would master. I griped and generally complained my way through the entire class (I am sure I was Pam's version of the worst student, yet one to be conquered and improved). Down on our knees, we were told to thrust our legs back, then up, then over the other leg, 'twenty times' she would say, then add on five more for good practice. And practice we did, through moans and groans and aches and pains until now I no longer whine when doing that particular exercise, no longer get leg cramps and want to call her a bitch.

I know people who hop from one spiritual "practice" to another, hoping that following this guru, doing this meditation pose, saying this mantra, will be the one thing to cause a break-through, a pathway to blisteringly brilliant enlightenment. But me, weighted down with the prospect of many more years of remodeling, have come to a different conclusion. One can perhaps improve their spiritual practice (and eventually achieve enlightenment) by living right where you are, in the moment. I can triumph over each unbalanced fitness ball in the Pilates class of life simply by choosing to see it differently.

Author Bios

Christiane Banta was a 2007 Macy's Most Inspiring Breast Cancer Survivor essay contest winner and was a memoir finalist in the 2008 PNWA Literary Contest. She has a Popular Fiction certificate from UW Continuing Education, where she also studied memoir writing. She lives in Seattle and is still with Jim.

Johna Beall, MA in Psychology, is working on a memoir of backpacking around the world at age 22, running an international business in Colombia, raising three kids in America and learning some tough lessons about love along the way. She lives with her husband and three rescued dogs near Seattle.

Paul Boardman lives in Seattle. By day he writes and at night works as a bartender, his second career after over two decades in international trade. He grew up in Japan, the son of missionaries. He can be found at *www.boardmawrites.com*

Michael Boudreaux lives with his partner, two dogs and two cats on a small farm in Washington State with plenty of room to run amok with things like dahlias. He is employed as a biochemist and continues to explore the gray line between memoir and fiction in his writing.

Abigail Carter wrote *The Alchemy of Loss: A Young Widow's Transformation* after her husband's death in the World Trade Center on 9/11. Toronto's *Globe and Mail* called it "Eloquent and honest," listing it as one of its top 100 books of 2008. Her work has appeared in *SELF*, *Reader's Digest Canada*, *MSN.com* and *MORE.com*. Abigail also writes a blog, The Alchemy of Loss (*www.alchemyofloss.com*) about a variety of subjects including widowhood, single parenting, dating, sex, dogs, and psychics.

Wendy Staley Colbert is writing a series of personal essays, on topics ranging from reconstructing her breasts, to losing two babies, to losing her brother to mental illness. She earned a B.A. degree in Journalism from Western Washington University, and holds certificates in Literary Fiction and Memoir.
For more information, see: *wendystaleycolbert.com*

Jennifer Crowder holds an MA in English from the University of North Carolina—Chapel Hill. After 17 years at a Seattle corporation, she took classes through the University of Washington Extension and began writing. One of her essays will be published in September, 2012 in the anthology *Side Effects*.

Carmen König D'Arcangelo has been writing since she was a little girl growing up in Germany. For the last 10 years she has woven writing into her professional life in human resources. In 2009 she graduated from the University of Washington Memoir program. She often sits in the kitchen with her 3 children doing 10 minute free writes.

Jean Engler is a creative woman who enjoys working in many mediums, fabric, paper, photography, and writing. Single with no children of her own, she is a fantastic aunt to ten nephews and five nieces. Her writing goal is to write family stories to pass on for the next generation.

Andrea Franzen is a proud Minnesota native who hates to be cold. She enjoys running, camping, traveling, snowboarding and well, writing. Her writing has appeared for several years in her blog called Two Star Hotel(*www.andreafranzen.blogspot.com*). She is currently penning her first memoir and plans to finish by 2012.

Laura Hebert hopes that by the time she and her husband get done with their ongoing do-it-yourself remodel project she will have achieved enlightenment, having been given ample opportunity for spiritual growth. Her zeal for writing was fostered in the Writing for Children and Memoir Certificate programs at the University of Washington.

Wendy Hinman has published stories in a number of sailing magazines and is nearing completion of a book about her 34,000-mile, seven-year adventure aboard a 31-foot boat with her husband. She is still married and still happens to like him. *wendyhinman.com*

Jennifer Landau lives in New York with her feisty boy, her elderly dog, and a betta fish she's managed to keep alive far longer than she intended. This essay—like everything—is for her son.

John Mace lives in Seattle, Washington. He graduated from Pacific Lutheran University, Antioch University and Washington School of Professional Psychology. John currently has a private practice in self-awareness and lectures nationally and internationally. *www.John-Mace.com.*

Lauren McGuire is writing a book, *The Keeper of Secret Sorrows*, about her brother's battle with schizophrenia. Her essay, "Haunted," will be published in 2012 in *Side Effects*, a Canadian anthology about the impact of mental illness on families. She is married and has two children.

Ashly Moore lives with her sweetheart of twenty years and two clever, talented children. She has been a writer all her life, but this is her first publication. In her free time, she likes to garden, play with her friends and look for exciting ways to physically exert herself.

Elizabeth Corcoran Murray publishes author interviews and resources in the Seattle area *Writers Connection,* found at *www.elizabethcorcoranmurray.com.* She has certificates in Generating Memoir and Literary Fiction from the University of Washington, as well as a Masters in Social Work. Elizabeth lives on an island in the Puget Sound with her husband, daughter, and frisky cat.

Peggy Nagae is an author with degrees in law, spiritual psychology and illumination sciences. She owns peggynagae consulting and coaches teams and leaders to achieve potent business results with greater grace and ease. Additionally, her work includes change, strategic planning, potentiating the human spirit at work, diversity and inclusion: *www.diversitycollaborative.com*

Theo Pauline Nestor edited the anthology *We Came to Say*. She is an instructor of the University of Washington Extension Program's yearlong course "Writing the Memoir" and also works with individual writers as a writing coach. She is the author of *How to Sleep Alone in a King-Size Bed* (Crown). Her next book, *Writing is My Drink: A Field Guide to Finding Your Own Voice*, is forthcoming from Simon and Schuster. Follow her blog at *WritingIsMyDrink.com*.

Rosemary Orr was born in Northern Ireland and went to medical school there. She came to the United States for her "been to America degree" and liked being here so much that she stayed in the country and became a citizen. She is a pediatric anesthesiologist in Seattle.

Heather Patrick is working on a memoir reflecting on her sailing trip from Seattle to New Zealand and her parallel journey from maiden to middle-age. A 1983 graduate of the University of Washington, Heather completed the UW's extension certificate program in memoir writing in 2009.

Natalie Singer worked for a decade as a journalist at newspapers around the West. She now writes essays and memoir on such arbitrary topics as the impermanence of family and her nature phobia. She lives with her husband and daughters in Seattle and can be found at *www. nataliesingerwrites.com*.

Eve M. Tai is a writer, yoga teacher and bon vivant. She lives in Seattle with her 3-legged pit bull, Olive. Her website is *www.writereve.com*.

Jeanne Verville has had careers in audiology, real estate and law. She is writing a memoir about the roles she played during years of cultural change. Her essays, *The First Step* and *My Fish Story*, appeared this year in *The Fallen Leaf Anthology*. Her guiding principle is *carpe diem*. jeanneverville@comcast.net.

Kellini Walter lives in Seattle with her two daughters, two dogs, and two cats. She has been a marketing professional for over twenty years. In addition to writing a memoir, she also brings her passion for written and spoken words into her job as an executive communications manager at Microsoft. *www.kellini.wordpress.com*.

Sue Wiedenfeld has lived in Seattle since 1986. She lives with her husband, fifteen-year-old son, and her 8 year-old Chihuahua, Pepper. She is a psychologist in private practice and began writing after attending a life coaching retreat at a ranch in Arizona in 2008. She has a longstanding interest in grief and loss.

Amber Wong is an environmental engineer who is a lot more fun than her profession would imply. Past publishing credits have keywords like "wastewater." Now she is avidly retooling to write about what she loves. She earned her bachelor's and master's degrees from Stanford University. She is married with two sons and two stepsons.